Journalistic Reading Book I

英语报刊选读系列教材

总主编 王嘉褆

英语报刊选读 第一册

主编 刘 雁

图书在版编目(CIP)数据

英语报刊选读.第一册/王嘉禔总主编;刘雁主编.—北京:北京大学出版社,2011.3
ISBN 978-7-301-18109-6

Ⅰ.①英… Ⅱ.①王… ②刘… Ⅲ.①英语-阅读教学-高等学校-教材 Ⅳ.①H319.4

中国版本图书馆CIP数据核字(2010)第232219号

书 名:	英语报刊选读(第一册)
著作责任者:	刘 雁 主编
责任编辑:	尹 璐 朱梅全 王业龙
标准书号:	ISBN 978-7-301-18109-6/H·2699
出版发行:	北京大学出版社
地 址:	北京市海淀区成府路205号 100871
网 址:	http://www.pup.cn
电 话:	邮购部 62752015 发行部 62750672 编辑部:62752027 出版部 62754962
电子邮箱:	law@pup.pku.edu.cn
印 刷 者:	北京富生印刷厂
经 销 者:	新华书店
	730毫米×980毫米 16开本 11.25印张 184千字
	2011年3月第1版 2019年1月第4次印刷
定 价:	20.00元

未经许可,不得以任何方式复制或抄袭本书之部分或全部内容。
版权所有 侵权必究
举报电话:010-62752024 电子邮箱:fd@pup.pku.edu.cn

编者说明

本套教材的编写,广泛借鉴了国内外优秀英语教材的编写经验,旨在通过原汁原味的外刊文章、鲜活生动的语言和多样的练习帮助学生扫除阅读英语报刊的障碍,培养阅读兴趣和良好的阅读习惯。本教材可供高等学校英语专业学生使用。

本套教材分为四册,每册十六个单元,选材既涉及与生活体验同质的校园、娱乐、体育方面,也有各类报刊中常见的医学、心理学、艺术、文化方面,在第三、四册我们还以国家为线索,选用了关于韩国、日本、印度、伊朗、伊拉克、巴基斯坦、以色列等热点问题较为集中的国家和地区。第一、二册每单元包含两篇文章,总字数控制在2000个单词以内;第三、四册包含两到三篇文章,总字数约为3000个单词。每个单元分三个部分,结构如下:

第一部分(Section A)是教学前的辅助材料,包括:

导读(Lead-in)介绍英语国家的主要报纸、杂志等,或简单讲解与本单元有关的背景知识。

热身问题(Warm-up Questions)集中体现在第一、二册,用几个与本单元相关的问题引出课文。

第二部分(Section B)是教材的课文部分,包含两至三篇相关题材的报道。其中第一、二册每单元两篇文章,每篇文章约为800—900个单词;第三、四册每单元两至三篇文章,每篇文章1000个单词以上。

第三部分(Section C)是教材的练习部分,分为词汇、句型和篇章三个类别。此部分参考答案请登录 http://www.shengdabooks.com 下载。

词汇练习(Vocabulary Builder)在第一、二册,词汇练习有根据上下文猜词、用原文中的生词填空、原文词组汉译英等形式;第三、四册的词汇练习采用生词与释义连线、近义词辨析、构词法练习等。

句型练习(Sentence Structure)在第一、二册,句型练习采用翻译长句的形式;

第三、四册则是将句子中的长句拆分为短句,再由学生将若干短句组合成长句。

篇章练习(Comprehension of the Texts)每册都设计了若干细节性或拓展性的问题,可供学生在课内或课外讨论。

本套教材坚持使用原汁原味的英语报刊文章,尽量不对原文进行编辑。我们认为,英语报刊阅读通常是带着生词的泛读,因此我们没有罗列生词表,也没有对课文进行注释。我们利用练习部分体现出文章的重点词汇,如一、二册的猜词、短语汉译英,又如三、四册的释义连线和近义词辨析等。由于我们的选材涵盖了英、美各大主流媒体的文章,为保持原文特色,没有对全书的英、美式拼写进行统一,望读者理解。

本套教材总主编为王嘉褆,第一、二册主编为刘雁,第三、四册主编为林玫。在教材编写过程中,我们得到了华东政法大学教务处、华东政法大学外语学院的关心和支持,也得到了北京大学出版社的大力帮助,在此一并致谢。

本书所选文章均已注明出处,因各种原因,未能联系上作者,敬请诸位作者与出版社或主编联系,以奉稿酬。

目录 Contents

Unit 1	Campus	(1)
Unit 2	Entertainment	(11)
Unit 3	Animal	(22)
Unit 4	Food	(34)
Unit 5	Crime	(44)
Unit 6	Disaster	(55)
Unit 7	Sports	(66)
Unit 8	Art	(76)
Unit 9	Economy	(87)
Unit 10	Ecology	(100)
Unit 11	Health	(110)
Unit 12	Automobile & Driving	(122)
Unit 13	Quality Problems	(133)
Unit 14	Shopping	(145)
Unit 15	Gun Control	(156)
Unit 16	Psychology	(165)

Unit 1

Campus

Section A Before Reading

Part One   Lead-in

Kaplan Test Prep and Admissions (www. kaptest. com), a division of Kaplan, Inc. , is a premier provider of educational and career services for individuals, schools and businesses. Established in 1938, Kaplan is the world leader in the test prep industry. With a comprehensive menu of online offerings and a complete array of books and software, Kaplan offers preparation for more than 90 standardized tests.

Newsweek (www. newsweek. com) is an American weekly newsmagazine published in New York City. It is distributed throughout the United States and internationally. It is the second largest news weekly magazine in the U. S. , having trailed *Time* in circulation and advertising revenue for most of its existence. *Newsweek* is published in four English language editions and 12 global editions written in the language of the circulation region. Recently, the magazine's owner The Washington Post Company has stated the publication has been losing profit. The company overhauled the magazine in May 2009, refocusing its content and using higher-quality paper, to target a smaller and more "elite audience" and to identify itself as a "thought leader. "

Newsweek-Kaplan College Guide: Combining the leadership of more than 70 years of college admissions expertise with the journalistic excellence of the nation's leading news magazine, *Newsweek*-Kaplan College Guide is published once a year, providing in-depth perspective into an increasingly complex college admissions process. The content of the Guide covers a variety of topics, from discussions on the benefits of community college, to the new options for students seeking a global education, student alcoholism, rise in online learning, the impact of Facebook on campus relationships, and more. The Guide is designed to help college-bound students and their families by illuminating issues, challenges and opportunities that await them all the way from the application process through their college senior year.

Part Two   Warm-up Questions

1. What do you plan to do at your first college year?

2. Which is more important to a successful college life, scores, friends, or extracurricular activities?

3. There is an employment problem in China now. What will you do in college to prepare yourself for a job when you graduate?

Section B   Texts Reading

Text A

Passions, Friends, and Great Profs

After you arrive on campus, the real decisions begin

http://www.newsweek.com/id/210895

By Sarah Starr   Aug. 12, 2009

1   For four years of high school, dreams of college life kept me persevering through what seemed like unbearable times of teenage torment. So when I got to college, I felt

a lot of pressure to make sure it was the best four years of my life. Although I made an excellent choice in Washington University in St. Louis, it was really the decisions I made once I arrived that made my college experience what I hoped it would be.

2　　Freshman year was chaotic. I made friends in an instant, only to stop hanging out with them days later. I felt lonely without people who knew me well. But when I looked around my freshman floor, I wasn't sure what "group" I belonged to. The answer proved to be no group. So I didn't try to force a bad fit and, at the same time, tried not to panic. I wound up with an eclectic collection of interesting and fun people who didn't fit neatly into any group either.

3　　Although I admit I sometimes forgot that education was the primary reason I was at college, I did learn that choosing my courses wisely was critical to my happiness. It was essential to check out the professors—read course evaluations, talk to former students—before committing, because it's the teacher who makes the course. I learned not to be seduced by clever course titles. If a boring prof teaches Guns, Gams, and Grass: The History of Violence, Sex, and Drugs in Pop Culture, the class will be little more than an opportunity to catch up on sleep. But if a great professor teaches History of Dirt, it's probably worth taking. A Human Evolution course that I reluctantly took to meet a science requirement proved to be an academic highlight because the professor was a compelling lecturer.

4　　Wash U, like most colleges, offers its students hundreds of opportunities to hear speakers, to see films, plays, and art exhibitions, or to go on free or heavily discounted trips. I am glad I took advantage—from the St. Louis Art Fair to a lecture on the crisis in Rwanda to the second-largest Mardi Gras celebration in the country.

5　　Extracurricular activities are one of the first things pushed on you when you arrive at college. Nearly everyone I know signed up for at least 10 clubs, and few kept up with more than one. Still, many did form close friendships or discovered an enduring passion. It doesn't, however, always work out smoothly. I joined the campus radio station as a DJ. After starting with a 2 a.m. Saturday show, I landed the Wednesday-at-4-p.m. slot, a time when people were actually listening. But two weeks into my new *Plastic Fantastic Radio* show, a student boss informed me that playing Janis Joplin revealed me as "too mainstream." I spent the next few weeks scouring stacks of indie garbage for appropriately obscure music before deciding that any radio station that failed to appreciate rock and roll was not for me.

6   Ultimately, it was the friendships that ensured my success at Wash U. To me, the key was finding a group that included a wide variety of tastes and temperaments. That requires being open to people with whom you might never have expected to get along. (Like, in my case, Republicans, a high-school homecoming queen, and a budding civil engineer.)

7   I certainly never believed I would become close friends with my freshman roommate. At first she spent all her spare time with her soccer teammates. We didn't have problems, but we barely spoke. Which was OK, because what does a big-city, East Coast girl like me have in common with a girl from the cornfields of Indiana?

8   To my surprise, it turned out to be quite a lot. One night, shortly after Thanksgiving break, we started sharing our high-school experiences and something clicked. From then on we were inseparable, and we remained roommates for the duration. Leaving Wash U proved a lot harder than starting there four years before.

Text B

The Case Against College Education

http://www.time.com/time/nation/article/0,8599,1967580,00.html
By Ramesh Ponnuru   Feb. 24, 2010

1   Even in these days of partisan rancor, there is a bipartisan consensus on the high value of postsecondary education. That more people should go to college is usually taken as a given. In his State of the Union address last month, President Obama echoed the words of countless high school guidance counselors around the country: "In this economy, a high school diploma no longer guarantees a good job." Virginia Governor Bob McDonnell, who gave the Republican response, concurred: "All Americans agree that a young person needs a world-class education to compete in the global economy."

2   The statistics seem to bear him out. People with college degrees make a lot more than people without them, and that difference has been growing. But does that

mean that we should help more kids go to college—or that we should make it easier for people who didn't go to college to make a living?

3   We may be close to maxing out on the first strategy. Our high college drop-out rate—40% of kids who enroll in college don't get a degree within six years—may be a sign that we're trying to push too many people who aren't suited for college to enroll. It has been estimated that, in 2007, most people in their 20s who had college degrees were not in jobs that required them: another sign that we are pushing kids into college who will not get much out of it but debt.

4   The benefits of putting more people in college are also oversold. Part of the college wage premium is an illusion. People who go to college are, on average, smarter than people who don't. In an economy that increasingly rewards intelligence, you'd expect college grads to pull ahead of the pack even if their diplomas signified nothing but their smarts. College must make many students more productive workers. But at least some of the apparent value of a college degree, and maybe a lot of it, reflects the fact that employers can use it as a rough measure of job applicants' intelligence and willingness to work hard.

5   We could probably increase the number of high school seniors who are ready to go to college—and likely to make it to graduation—if we made the K-12 system more academically rigorous. But let's face it: college isn't for everyone, especially if it takes the form of four years of going to classes on a campus.

6   To talk about college this way may sound élitist. It may even sound philistine, since the purpose of a liberal-arts education is to produce well-rounded citizens rather

than productive workers. But perhaps it is more foolishly élitist to think that going to school until age 22 is necessary to being well-rounded, or to tell millions of kids that their future depends on performing a task that only a minority of them can actually accomplish.

7 The good news is that there have never been more alternatives to the traditional college. Some of these will no doubt be discussed by a panel of education experts on Feb. 26 at the National Press Club, a debate that will be aired on PBS. Online learning is more flexible and affordable than the brick-and-mortar model of higher education. Certification tests could be developed so that in many occupations employers could get more useful knowledge about a job applicant than whether he has a degree. Career and technical education could be expanded at a fraction of the cost of college subsidies. Occupational licensure rules could be relaxed to create opportunities for people without formal education.

8 It is absurd that people have to get college degrees to be considered for good jobs in hotel management or accounting—or journalism. It is inefficient, both because it wastes a lot of money and because it locks people who would have done good work out of some jobs. The tight connection between college degrees and economic success may be a nearly unquestioned part of our social order. Future generations may look back and shudder at the cruelty of it.

Section C After Reading

I. *Vocabulary Builder*

1. Do NOT consult the dictionary, and guess the meanings of the underlined words from **Text A** by the context, word formation, grammar, general knowledge, or any other skills you can rely on.

 1) Newscasts continued to broadcast images of the ***chaotic*** minutes after the shooting.

 2) Our ***primary*** concern is to provide the refugees with food and healthcare.

 3) A majority of law school graduates are ***seduced*** by the huge salaries offered by large firms.

4) We were looking forward to seeing the pyramids, which promised to be the *highlight* *of our trip.*

5) In any case, lawyers are typically *reluctant* to take on the cases that are time-consuming and difficult.

6) The film was so *compelling* I could scarcely take my eyes off the screen for a second.

7) Nationwide studies *reveal* that consumers spend an average 33 percent more, or $36, on groceries each week.

8) The *mainstream* political parties are losing support to smaller, more radical organizations.

9) During the recession period, a second income, with no doubt, is *critical* to a family's well-being.

10) The process of biological *evolution* has taken billions of years.

2. Read through **Text B** and find the English counterparts of the following Chinese words or phrases.

1) 两党共识
2) 高中学历
3) 辍学率
4) 大学(毕业生)额外工资
5) 从幼儿园到12年制(学校教育)的体系
6) 学术方面更严格
7) 全面发展的公民
8) 资格证书考试
9) 职业技术教育

3. Study the following synonyms and fill in each of the blanks with one from the box, change forms when necessary.

If you want to say 坚持, you can use:

a) **persist**: [vi.] *formal to continue to do something, especially something bad that you have been warned not to do, or something difficult that other people do not want you to do*

b) **persevere**: [vi.] *to continue trying to do something in a very patient and determined way, in spite of difficulties*

c) **insist**: [vi., vt.] *to say firmly that someone must do something or that something must happen*

1) He didn't know any English, but he _____ and became a good student.
2) He _____ in smoking even after having a heart attack.
3) He was a religious man who _____ his children went to church every Sunday.
4) The man _____ on helping me find a taxi even though I told him I didn't need any help.
5) When a country is able to _____ with/in reforms, the result can be a return to economic stability.

If you want to say *something painful or unpleasant that you suffer*, you can use:

> a) **torment**: [cn., un.] behavior or situations that are comical are funny in an odd or unexpected way, although they are not usually intended to be
>
> b) **plight**: [singular noun] a difficult and unpleasant situation, in which people are suffering a lot and that makes you feel great sympathy for them
>
> c) **agony**: [un.] a very sad, difficult, and unpleasant situation in which people suffer a lot, especially over a long time
>
> d) **adversity**: [un.] a situation in which you have continuing difficulties that seem to be caused by bad luck

6) In the book she describes the _____ of watching her child die.
7) They have suffered more than their fair share of _____ and managed to overcome it every time.
8) It's difficult for us to understand the _____ the hostages are going through.
9) A new report exposes the _____ of skilled nurses, who work long hours for very low rates of pay.

Unit 1
Campus

If you want to say 确保, you can use:

a) **insure**: [vi., vt.] to buy insurance so that you will receive money if something bad happens to you, your family, your possessions etc.

b) **ensure**: [vt.] also **insure** AmE. To do something in order to be certain that something will happen in the way you want it to

c) **assure**: [vt.] to tell someone that something will definitely happen or is definitely true, so that they are less worried or more confident

d) **reassure**: [vt.] to make someone feel less worried or frightened about a situation, for example by being friendly to them or by telling them there is nothing to worry about

10) I tried to _____ her that she had made the right decision in turning down the job.

11) To _____ accuracy, three consultants worked closely with the producer during filming.

12) You should _____ the painting for at least £100,000.

13) It is important to _____ that universities have enough funds to carry out important research.

14) The doctor _____ me that I wouldn't feel any pain.

II. Sentence Translation

1. Although I made an excellent choice in Washington University in St. Louis, it was really the decisions I made once I arrived that made my college experience what I hoped it would be. (Para. 1, Text A)

_____

_____

2. A Human Evolution course that I reluctantly took to meet a science requirement proved to be an academic highlight because the professor was a compelling lecturer. (Para. 3, Text A)

_____

3. I spent the next few weeks scouring stacks of indie garbage for appropriately obscure music before deciding that any radio station that failed to appreciate rock and roll was not for me. (Para. 5, Text A)

4. It has been estimated that, in 2007, most people in their 20s who had college degrees were not in jobs that required them: another sign that we are pushing kids into college who will not get much out of it but debt. (Para. 3, Text B)

5. But at least some of the apparent value of a college degree, and maybe a lot of it, reflects the fact that employers can use it as a rough measure of job applicants' intelligence and willingness to work hard. (Para. 4, Text B)

III. Comprehension of the Texts

Answer the following questions.

Questions 1—4 are for Text A:

1) Why was the author so anxious to make his college life perfect?
2) Why did the author find her first year in college was a mess?
3) Why are two lecture titles provided in Paragraph 3?
4) What is essential to make friends with people according to the author?

Questions 5—8 are for Text B:

5) Why are Obama and Bob McDonnell mentioned in Paragraph 1?
6) How many indications are given to illustrate the author's argument in Paragraph 3? And what are they?
7) What is the significance of a college diploma for the employers?
8) How many alternatives are there to the conventional college education? And what are they?

Unit 2

Entertainment

Section A Before Reading

Part One Lead-in

BusinessWeek is a business magazine first published in 1929 by McGraw-Hill Publishing company. Its primary competitors in the national business magazine category are Fortune and Forbes, which are published bi-weekly. From 1975, it carried more advertising pages annually than any magazine in the United States, and in the mid-1990s its circulation was more than one million worldwide. Like nearly all magazines, *BusinessWeek* has suffered from a decline in advertising during the late-2000s recession. As of July 2009, McGraw-Hill is reportedly trying to sell *BusinessWeek* and has hired Evercore Partners to conduct the sale. Because of the magazine's liabilities it has been suggested that it may change hands for the nominal price of $1 to an investor who is willing to incur losses turning the magazine around.

The Walt Disney Company, often simply known as Disney, is the largest media and entertainment conglomerate in the world, known for its family-friendly products. Founded on October 16, 1923, by brothers Walt Disney and Roy Disney as an animation studio, it has become one of the biggest Hollywood studios, and owner and licensor of eleven theme parks and several television networks, including ABC and ESPN. Disney's corporate headquarters and primary production facilities are located at The Walt Disney Studios in Burbank, California. The company has been a component of the Dow Jones Industrial Average since May 6, 1991. Mickey Mouse serves as the official mascot of The Walt Disney Company.

Part Two Warm-up Questions

1. Who's your favorite cartoon character, spider-man, X-men, or anyone else? Why?

2. Which do you think is the most successful animated cartoon company in America? Why?

3. Use three adjectives to describe Michael Jackson, and make your own comments on this controversial figure.

Section B Texts Reading

Text A

Disney to Buy Marvel for $4 Billion

The deal will give Disney a host of strong characters—Spider-Man, X-Men, and others—that it can sell to teen boys

http://www.businessweek.com/bwdaily/dnflash/content/aug2009/db20090831_005947.htm

By Ronald Grover Aug. 31, 2009

1   Walt Disney's (DIS) purchase of Marvel Entertainment (MVL) for $4 billion in cash and stock, announced on Aug. 31, clearly gives Disney another strong brand. But just as important, it gives it a brand to sell to teen boys, which has remained a lingering weakness for the company that sells tons of Hannah Montana

clothes to preteen girls and Mickey and Minnie toys to younger children.

2 Through its history, Disney had been one of Hollywood's biggest brand hunters, with a collection of acquisitions that have included Winnie the Pooh, ESPN, and the ABC TV network. The deal also represents the latest step in the march by Disney CEO Bob Iger, who took over the top job in 2005, to build out the company that he inherited from former top Disney executive Michael Eisner. Just months after taking the job, Iger engineered the $6 billion acquisition of Pixar, the computer animation powerhouse headed by Apple's Steve Jobs, with whom Eisner had feuded. Earlier this year, Iger cut a distribution deal with Steven Spielberg's newly recreated DreamWorks film studio, after Spielberg had left Paramount (VIAB) and nearly signed with Universal Pictures (GE).

3 "This transaction combines Marvel's strong global brand and world-renowned library of characters, including Iron Man, Spider-Man, X-Men, Captain America, Fantastic Four, and Thor, with Disney's creative skills, unparalleled global portfolio of entertainment properties, and a business structure that maximizes the value of creative properties across multiple platforms and territories," Iger said in announcing the transaction.

A Valuable Combo

4 Disney already features Marvel shows that include Spider-Man, X-Men, and The Incredible Hulk on its newly christened all-boys cable channel, Disney XD. The deal does present one problem to future exploitation of some Marvel properties, however. Marvel has made movies of some of its most profitable franchises for other studios—Spider-Man at Sony (SNE) and Iron Man with Paramount—and has licensed its properties widely throughout the entertainment world. It currently licenses its characters, for instance, so that Spider-Man appears at Universal Studio theme parks in Japan and in Orlando, where it has created a Marvel Super Hero Island.

5 Still, Marvel has traditionally cut handsome deals for itself with those properties, and Disney gets a huge upside from a library of more than 5,000 other characters.

6 The deal, which valued Marvel at $50 a share, represents a 28% premium to

Marvel's stock price, which closed on Aug. 28 at $38.65. Under the arrangement, Marvel will continue to be operated by longtime President and CEO Ike Perlmutter, who will oversee the brand but will not join the Disney board. Perlmutter, who owns 37% of Marvel, also stands to reap more than $1.5 billion in cash and stock from the Disney purchase. After the deal is completed—Disney said it is subject to federal antitrust review—Perlmutter would control 22 million Disney shares, or about 1.4% of Disney's stock.

7   Marvel shares jumped $10.19, or 26%, to $48.84 in the first half hour of trading. Disney shares were off 36 ¢, or 1.3%, to $26.48.

Grover is Los Angeles bureau chief for BusinessWeek.

Text B

Death of A Showman

Michael Jackson made great pop records, lurid headlines and lots of money

http://www.economist.com/books/displaystory.cfm?story_id=13919497
From Economist.com June 26, 2009

1   For a life so extraordinary the manner of Michael Jackson's passing on Thursday June 25 was utterly banal: a middle-aged man succumbing to an apparent heart-attack. (There was speculation that an alleged dependency on prescription painkillers may have been a contributing factor.) During his progress from child prodigy to the

self-styled "King of Pop" and, more recently, an eccentric semi-recluse, no part of Mr Jackson's private life had given any other hint of normality. But behind the mask that plastic surgeons had made of his face was a keen brain for wringing cash out of pop music—and for spending it.

2   Mr Jackson first performed on stage at the age of six, accompanying his four older brothers. The Jackson Five, under the strict stewardship of their manager and father, signed to Motown Records in the late 1960s and began producing a string of hit records—a sequence of success that Mr Jackson continued in a 30-year solo recording career. It is reckoned that his final tally of album sales is around 750m—the most that any artist has sold. And one of those, "Thriller", released in 1982, became the most successful yet seen, <u>shifting</u> 65m units. This record may well remain unchallenged: sales of albums have suffered as pop fans these days prefer downloading individual tracks from the internet.

3   The length of Mr Jackson's career ensured that he experienced, popularised and even pioneered many of the techniques that help artists to profit from their musical talents. At the beginning of his career, touring was a vital component of performers' incomes, though a shift to earning money from selling records was well under way. By its peak, in the 1980s, touring had come to be seen by the music industry as a loss-making promotional tool to shift albums.

4   Mr Jackson did not invent the pop promotional video, as he is sometimes credited with doing. But he took this art form to new heights with the lavishly expensive video he made in 1983 for the title track of the "Thriller" album. He brought in one of Hollywood's top directors, John Landis (best known for "The Blues Brothers"), and spent an unprecedented $500,000 on the 14-minute miniature epic. But it was money well spent: the launch of MTV, two years earlier, whose format was being copied by other broadcasters, meant that videos had rapidly become one of the most valuable tools for marketing recorded music, and more cost-effective than concert tours. The "Thriller" video was broadcast incessantly all around the world, pumping up the album's sales.

5   At the height of his success Mr Jackson and his team of managers made the shrewd calculation that the value of pop music was wrapped up in the publishing

rights to songs just as much as in record sales. In 1985 he paid $47.5m for ATV Music, which owned the copyrights to most of the Beatles' songs. Ten years later he sold half his interest for $150m to Sony. The value of his stake was probably around $500m when he died. This was roughly equal to the upper estimates of the debts he was struggling to refinance, which he had amassed funding his increasingly bizarre style of living.

6   Despite his vast earnings Mr Jackson was forced to borrow huge sums against his stake in ATV and his future earnings (recently reckoned to be about $19m a year) to pay for his huge shopping sprees and the upkeep of "Neverland", his ranch in California. Last year he announced plans for a long series of concerts in London to boost his income and pay off his creditors. Playing live has re-emerged as the way to make money from pop as falling sales, rampant piracy and digital distribution have slashed revenues from recorded music.

7   Despite having built himself an extravagant fun palace, with its own zoo, fairground and elaborate topiary, Mr Jackson cut an increasingly lost and lonely figure in his later years. Though twice married and with three children, his closest relationships appeared to be with a chimpanzee and a succession of young boys. The questions raised by these unusual friendships continued to <u>hang in the air</u> until his death. He was acquitted in a Californian court in 2005 on charges of molesting one 13-year-old boy but reportedly paid $20m out of court in 1994 to <u>head off</u> other allegations of child abuse.

8   His status as a pop genius may well always be tainted by the strangeness of the life he chose to lead. Elvis Presley, still the unchallenged King of Rock'n'Roll, is increasingly remembered for his music, as memories fade of his own unusual private life. Mr Jackson would doubtless have craved to be held in the same public awe and affection (his dynastic ambitions even stretched to a brief marriage with Lisa Marie, Presley's only child). But, sadly, for now he will be remembered by many as "Wacko Jacko" rather than the King of Pop.

Section C After Reading

I. Vocabulary Builder

1. Do NOT consult the dictionary, and guess the meanings of the underlined words by the context, word formation, grammar, general knowledge, or any other skills you can rely on.

   The following items are for Text A:
   1) Now let the chocolate melt slowly in your mouth and enjoy the ***lingering*** tastes.
   2) To teach ***preteen*** boys, rich dad kept everything simple, using as many pictures as possible, as few words as possible, and no numbers for years.
   3) After raising the money, the hospital was able to ***build out*** a whole new section.
   4) Poison symbolizes human society's tendency to poison good things and make them fatal, just as the pointless Capulet-Montague ***feud*** turns Romeo and Juliet's love to poison.
   5) The hotel is not responsible for any loss or damage to guests' personal ***property***.
   6) The Shanghai Grand Theater is ***featuring*** the film *The Founding of a Republic* this week.
   7) Many towns were full of shopping malls and fast-food ***franchises***.
   8) The deal, which valued Marvel at $50 a share, represents a 28% ***premium*** to Marvel's stock price, which closed on Aug. 28 at $38.65.

   The following items are for Text B:
   9) The witness's statement was pure ***speculation***. It's not based on any facts, but from his guess.
   10) Much of Manchester United's success can be ***credited*** to their manager.
   11) Are the changes enough to transform more non-believers into Corvette buyers and ***pump*** sales back ***up***, as Chevrolet hopes?

12) Pickpocketing is so *rampant* on this street that no one dare say anything when they saw a thief put his hand into a young girl's backpack.

2. Complete the sentences using words given in the box, change forms when necessary.

cut a deal	incessant	inherit	unparalleled	platform
portfolios	transaction	reckoned	territory	prescription

1) Good as it is to _____ a library, it is better to collect one.

2) After six months of negotiations the two airlines announced today they have _____ to share their domestic and international routes and increase their traffic to Europe and Asia.

3) In view of our longstanding business relationship, we can conclude the _____.

4) The recent economic recession is _____ since the 1930s.

5) Financial institutions act as intermediaries between lenders and borrowers, and manage their own asset _____.

6) Miller had accidentally crossed into Iraqi _____ and was arrested for spying.

7) "The deal provides us with a(n) _____ for expansion into new markets," Weldon said.

8) If you are pregnant, it's hard to get a(n) _____ for sleeping pills from the doctor.

9) Moving house is _____ to be nearly as stressful as divorce.

10) Thunder exploded, roll after roll after roll, so that there seemed to be no gap between but only a(n) _____ bombardment.

II. Sentence Translation

1. But just as important, it gives it a brand to sell to teen boys, which has remained a lingering weakness for the company that sells tons of Hannah Montana clothes to preteen girls and Mickey and Minnie toys to younger children. (Para. 1, Text A)

2. This transaction combines Marvel's strong global brand and world-renowned library of characters, including Iron Man, Spider-Man, X-Men, Captain America, Fantastic Four, and Thor, with Disney's creative skills, unparalleled global portfolio of entertainment properties, and a business structure that maximizes the value of creative properties across multiple platforms and territories. (Para. 3, Text A)

3. The length of Mr Jackson's career ensured that he experienced, popularised and even pioneered many of the techniques that help artists to profit from their musical talents. (Para. 3, Text B)

4. At the height of his success Mr Jackson and his team of managers made the shrewd calculation that the value of pop music was wrapped up in the publishing rights to songs just as much as in record sales. (Para. 5, Text B)

5. Playing live has re-emerged as the way to make money from pop as falling sales, rampant piracy and digital distribution have slashed revenues from recorded music. (Para. 6, Text B)

III. Comprehension of the Texts

Answer the following questions, or choose the best answer.

Questions 1—5 are for Text A:

1. What is the business significance for Walt Disney to purchase Marvel Entertainment?

2. What is the business tradition of Disney company?

3. What are the building-out moves Iger made after he took over Disney?

4. Why there might be some trouble for Disney to use Marvel's certain properties in the future?

5. Did Marvel suffer a financial loss due to Disney's acquisition?

Questions 6—14 are for Text B:

6. In sentence "*By its peak, in the 1980s, touring had come to be seen by the music industry as a loss-making promotional tool to shift albums,*" (Para. 3) the underlined "its" refers to _____.

   A. touring
   B. selling records
   C. 1980s
   D. Jackson's career

7. The underlined word "shift" in Para. 2 reappears in Para. 3. Do they share the same meaning?

8. Which of the following statement is true?

   A. Jackson launched MTV two years earlier than anyone else.
   B. Jackson made great contribution to the development of music industry because he invented MTV.
   C. Jackson did not invent the pop promotional video, though he invented MTV.
   D. Jackson is the person that pushed the MTV to a new level.

9. In sentence "*This was roughly equal to the upper estimates of the debts he was struggling to refinance, which he had **amassed** funding his increasingly bizarre style of living,*" (Para. 5) which is the object of the shadowed verb "amass"?

   A. funding
   B. estimates
   C. debts
   D. style of living

10. Why Jackson was reduced to borrow money from his financial assets?

11. The underlined phrase "hang in the air" means _____. (Para. 7)

    A. to remain unexplained
    B. to be reported by the newspaper and magazines
    C. to be broadcasted through radio and TV
    D. to be blamed and distorted by the public

12. The underlined phrase "head off" means _____. (Para. 7)

    A. to leave to go to another place

B. to prevent something from happening

C. to stop someone going somewhere by moving in front of them

D. to be in charge of a team, government, organization etc.

13. Why Elvis Presley is mentioned in Paragraph 8?
14. What is the author's attitude toward Michael Jackson?

  A. Positive   B. Ironic

  C. Neutral   D. Critical

Unit 3

Animal

Section A Before Reading

Part One Lead-in

Time: Major American weekly newsmagazine that is published in New York City. *Time* was the creation of two young journalists, Henry R. Luce and Briton Hadden, who wanted to start a magazine that would inform busy readers in a systematic, concise, and well-organized manner about current events in the United States and the rest of the world. With Hadden as editor and Luce as business manager, they brought out the first issue on March 3, 1923. *Time*'s format, which became standard for most other general newsmagazines, consisted of dozens of short articles tersely summarizing information on subjects of importance and general interest and arranged in "departments" covering such fields as national and international affairs, business, education, science, medicine, law, religion, sports, books, and the arts. *Time* had attained a circulation of more than 175,000 by 1927, and it became the most influential newsmagazine in the United States. After Hadden's death in 1929, Luce remained the editor and guiding force behind the magazine until 1964, when he assumed the title of editorial chairman of Time Inc., the magazine's publisher. *Time* long reflected Luce's moderately conservative political viewpoint. By the 1970s, however, the magazine had assumed a more neutral, centrist stance in the tone of its reportage. From the 1970s to the end of the 20th century, the magazine's circulation hovered just above four million, significantly higher than its rivals, *Newsweek* and *U. S. News & World Report*. *Time* also appears in several foreign-language editions.

Part Two Warm-up Questions

1. Name a few endangered animals and discuss the ways to protect them.

2. Which kind of dogs do you like, the small-sized, good-tempered ones or the big-sized aggressive ones? Why?

3. What law or regulation will you propose to prevent dog from biting people if you were a member of National People's Congress?

Section B Texts Reading

Text A

Top 10 Animal Stories of 2008

http://www.time.com/time/specials/2008/top10/article/0,30583,1855948_1864552,00.html
By Frances Romero   2009

1. A big victory in the fight against cruelty to farm animals

California's Proposition 2, otherwise known as the Standards for Confining Farm Animals Initiative, was approved by a 63% majority, which means that by 2015, egg-laying chickens, veal calves and pregnant pigs will have to be given enough room to stand up, turn around, lie down, and extend their limbs. Opponents of the measure had argued that the requirements will force egg producers in particular to increase prices and risk losing more business to out-of-state farmers who aren't subject to the new law. But a study by the University of California-Riverside put the likely cost increase at one cent per egg, a price 63% of California voters appear willing to pay.

2. White House Pets, Part 1: Electing a new First Pup

Of all the things that Barack Obama vowed to do during his campaign for the presidency, the one that will most certainly be fulfilled is his promise to his two daughters to get a puppy. In his first post-election press conference, Obama said that figuring out what kind of dog to get had become "a major issue." And, boy, was he right about that. Entire websites were created to weigh in on which breed the Obamas should take to the White House. Some 50,000 people signed a petition urging the family to get a dog from a shelter. Obama took the suggestion to heart, but reminded everyone of 10-year-old Malia's allergies, which he said complicate the prospect of adopting "mutts like me". At presidentialpup.com, more than 42,000 people cast votes for five hypoallergenic breeds that the American Kennel Club thought would be a good choice for the Obamas. The poodle won, but no word yet on whether the Obamas will take them up on the advice.

3. White House Pets, Part 2: President's Dog Bites Man!

New rule for political reporters: Don't try to pet the dog of a man with a 23% approval rating. That advice came too late for Reuters reporter Jon Decker, who after delivering a live report from the White House for MSNBC, spotted the first dog, Barney. The usually affable Scottish terrier, evidently fed up with the recent GOP electoral drubbings, was not in the mood to be petted, but pet Decker did. Barney, in turn, responded like dogs do, biting the reporter's finger. Decker, to his credit, reacted with no four-letter words and only three other, very discreet ones: "That's not good." The reporter's finger was treated, the offending dog was presumably scolded—and democracy endured.

4. Whales lose Supreme Court case

In November the Supreme Court shocked no one with a ruling that national security takes precedence over wildlife protection. The decision lightened restrictions—levied by a federal judge in Los Angeles—on the use of sonar during Navy training exercises. Studies have shown that sonar pulses damage the hearing organs of whales and dolphins and can also hinder their ability to mate, find food and navigate. Some sonar pulses appear to have caused whales to strand themselves on shore, with necropsies finding signs of internal bleeding near their ears. While the Navy—which says its voluntary safeguards protect marine mammals by reducing sonar when whales or dolphins are spotted nearby—won the right to continue its training off the Southern California coast, environmentalists claimed a partial victory since the ruling did not exempt the Navy from having to prepare an environmental impact report for future exercises.

5. Another case of elephant herpes

In November, 2-year-old Mac became the sixth endangered Asian elephant born or kept at the Houston Zoo to die of elephant herpes since 2000. The precocious Mac had become one of the zoo's most popular animals, entertaining visitors by dancing, playing windpipes and standing on his head. His illness came on suddenly and vets, who know little about the virus other than that it is not sexually transmitted, were unable to save him. News of his death prompted People for the Ethical Treatment of Animals to call for an end to the zoo's elephant breeding program. But zoo officials responded that the virus is latent in elephants in the wild as well as in captivity and that its researchers were helping search for a cure.

6. Weirdest foreclosure victim: a 44-lb. cat

This colossal kitty, known as Prince Chunk, has had his 15 minutes for sure. Actually, about 10 of those minutes were spent under the guise of Princess Chunk before people realized the 44-lb. cat was a boy. The fatty feline, who is about two pounds shy of the world record for heaviest cat, got a big heave-ho from his owner in New Jersey when she lost her home to foreclosure and could no longer afford to feed him. She gave the cat to a friend, who in turn gave him to an animal shelter. His astounding girth helped the newly nicknamed Prince Chunk (his previous owner called him Powder) make his way on to *Good Morning America*, *Live with Regis and Kelly* and *Fox News*. And the media blitz worked like a charm: more than 400 families applied to adopt him, and he was quickly placed in a New Jersey home—and on a low-carb diet.

7. World's longest insect

Things to consider when planning a trip to Borneo: beautiful beaches, amazing culture, and big-time bugs. In October, British scientists identified the Phobaeticus chani as the longest insect in the world. The new species of stick-insect—nicknamed

"Chan's megastick" after the Malaysian amateur naturalist, Datuk Chan Chew Lun, who donated it to London's Natural History Museum—measures 22 inches long with its legs fully extended. Its body spans 14 of those inches. And what can these long fellows do? Paul Brock, a scientific associate of the British museum told the Associated Press, "Their main defense is basically hanging around, looking like a twig."

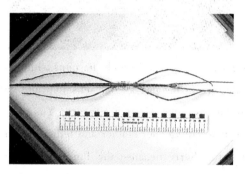

8. Monkeys pay for sex

A study published in *Animal Behavior* found that male long-tailed macaques in Indonesia traded grooming services for sex with females. The boys even paid upfront. And the lady macaques? Well, they held up their end of the deal, too. Female sexual activity more than doubled—from an average of 1.5 times an hour to 3.5 times—after a good grooming. The researchers also noted that the going rate, i.e., the amount of time males spent nit-picking, dwindled as the number of available females went up.

9. Monkeys wait tables, too

Another captivating macaque story! What can't these creatures do?!? Grooming, sexual favors and now food service. Video of simians serving drinks and hot towels in a Japanese restaurant became a hit on YouTube, where a news clip circulated in which the restaurant owner, Kaoru Otsuka, said he did not teach the monkeys waiting skills. Apparently, they learned by observing humans. Although the macaques work only two hours a day, they never get any days off. Two words: monkey union.

10. Puppycam

In years past, the big obsession was with pandacams. But 2008 went to the dogs. Animal lovers flocked to see streaming video of six baby Shiba Inus, whose

owners set up a live feed so they could watch the pups while they were at work. In a matter of days, the Puppycam became a viral sensation and captivated thousands of people for hour upon hour of puppy-viewing pleasure. You probably aren't even reading this right now. You're calling your mother and telling her to look at the cute little puppies. But you'd better hurry because the fun is about to end. The pups are scheduled to be divvied out to new owners starting in early December.

Text B

Dangerous Dogs in Denmark

Shoot the puppy! Danes turn on their former best friend

http://www.economist.com/world/europe/displaystory.cfm?story_id=14273944
From *The Economist* Aug. 20, 2009

1 Dogs, not recession or unemployment, are the biggest problem facing Denmark this summer, or so you would think from all the fuss about them. At his Liberal party's summertime get-together on the Faroe Islands, the prime minister, Lars Lokke Rasmussen, solemnly promised a new law to ban aggressive breeds of dog. "We don't want a society", he said with furrowed brow, "where you cannot go walking with your child or your poodle without risking an attack."

2 Things might seem to be going that way. According to the Danish Kennel Club, the kingdom's population of fighting breeds such as pit-bull terriers, mastiffs and rottweilers has risen from 1,000 to 20,000 in the past five years. The incidence of attacks, mostly on other pets, has grown accordingly. Denmark's national news agen-

cy, Ritzau, says there is a violent incident about once a fortnight. Several people have been mauled, though deaths so far have been confined to cats, rabbits and small dogs. Still, widespread worries that the next attack could kill a citizen have pushed man's erstwhile best friend to the top of the political agenda.

3 However, the prime minister's ringing proclamation was followed by a realisation that a ban on certain breeds—such as Britain introduced—might not work. Fanciers of muscular hounds with big jaws could circumnavigate the law by crossing, say, a mastiff with a pit bull, to create a perfectly legal canine nasty (as, indeed, has happened in Britain).

4 To meet the difficulty, Flemming Moller, a veterinarian who took over the parliamentary seat vacated when the former prime minister, Anders Fogh Rasmussen, went off to run NATO, proposed a logical, if drastic, solution: kill all mongrels. Mr Moller claims this is the only way to eliminate aggressive traits from the doggy gene pool. Only dogs registered in the national stud book have a record of their parentage and genetic traits. Other puppies, he says, could be the products of anything from joyful encounters in leafy suburbs to deliberate breeding by thugs. With some 40,000 mongrels born in Denmark every year, a mass cull of mutts would reach alarming proportions. Mr Moller is prepared for the backlash: "We will surely see lots of press photos of sweet little puppies being put down but we must be determined,"

he says unflinchingly.

5   Happily for the puppies, Mr Moller's idea has won little support. One outraged politician from the junior partner in the coalition, the conservatives, said he would "reach for his shotgun" if Mr Moller came calling. Indignant comments about Nazis and racial cleansing have swamped online forums. All of which leaves the government's attempt to rein in dangerous dogs looking like, well, a dog's dinner.

Section C   After Reading

I. Vocabulary Builder

1. Read through Text A and B and find the English counterparts of the following Chinese words or phrases.

   The following items are for Text A:

   1) 蛋鸡   2) 伸展四肢
   3) 不受新法制约   4) 履行承诺
   5) （狗的）品种   6) 签名请愿
   7) 投票   8) 进行现场报道
   9) 国家安全优于野生动物保护   10) 放松约束
   11) 倒立   12) （疾病）通过性传播
   13) 媒体闪电战   14) 美联社
   15) 伺候进餐   16) 分送给新主人

   The following items are for Text B:

   17) 紧锁的眉头   18) 国家新闻社
   19) 响亮的宣言   20) 对强烈反对作好准备

2. Complete the sentences using words given in the box, change forms when necessary.

allergy	be under the guise of	breed	captivating
confine	discreet	dwindle	eliminate
latent	obsession	prompt	weigh in

1) The current _____ with exam results is actually harming children's education.
2) A(n) _____ is an adverse reaction of the body to certain substances.
3) People might gossip if we arrived together. It would be much more _____ for us to go there separately.
4) The now responsibilities drew out his _____ talents.
5) The judge has _____ the jury to their hotel until after the verdict.
6) Somewhere inside a piano was being played, not very well but with a(n) _____ enthusiasm.
7) The country's foreign currency reserves have _____ over the past few years.
8) They operated a drug-smuggling business _____ an employment agency.
9) Her mother's accident _____ her to renew her insurance.
10) The new Transport Secretary, Stephen Byers, _____ with a demand that the industry should improve its performance.
11) The credit card _____ the need for cash or cheques.
12) But success in this world seems to _____ envy which, in its turn, can breed hostility.

II. Sentence Translation

1. While the Navy—which says its voluntary safeguards protect marine mammals by reducing sonar when whales or dolphins are spotted nearby—won the right to continue its training off the Southern California coast, environmentalists claimed a partial victory since the ruling did not exempt the Navy from having to prepare an environmental impact report for future exercises. (Story 4, Text A)

_____

_____

2. Still, widespread worries that the next attack could kill a citizen have pushed man's erstwhile best friend to the top of the political agenda. (Para. 2, Text B)

_____

_____

3. Fanciers of muscular hounds with big jaws could circumnavigate the law by crossing, say, a mastiff with a pit bull, to create a perfectly legal canine nasty (as, indeed, has happened in Britain). (Para. 3, Text B)

_____

4. Other puppies, he says, could be the products of anything from joyful encounters in leafy suburbs to deliberate breeding by thugs. (Para. 4, Text B)

_____

5. With some 40,000 mongrels born in Denmark every year, a mass cull of mutts would reach alarming **proportions**. (Para. 4, Text B)

_____

III. Comprehension of the Texts

Answer the following questions, or judge the given statements true or false.

Questions 1—12 are for Text A:

1. What are people's attitudes toward California's Proposition 2?
2. What does "out-of-state farmers" mean?
3. Will President Obama adopt a dog from the shelter?
4. Who does "a man with a 23% approval rating" in story 3 refer to?
5. Why the Reuters reporter was bitten by the first dog?
6. What are the damages the sonar pulse will cause to the sea mammals?
7. Will elephant Mac survive if he lived in the jungle rather than the zoo? Why?
8. Prince Chunk was the second heaviest cat in the world, which made him very shy. (T/F)(Story 6)
9. How do the world's longest insects defend themselves?
10. What service do the male macaques offer to exchange sex with females?
11. What are the other two synonyms of the word "monkey"? (Story 9)
12. How can the owners know the condition of the puppies when they are not at home?

Questions 13—15 are for Text B:

13. How often is there an incident caused by the aggressive breeds of dog?
14. According to Mr Moller, what is the foundation of his kill-all-mongrel proposal?
15. What are the comments on Mr Moller's proposal on the Internet?

Unit 4

Food

Section A Before Reading

Part One Lead-in

USA Today (trademarked as USA TODAY in capitals) is a national American daily newspaper published by the Gannett Company. It was founded by Al Neuharth. The paper has the widest circulation of any newspaper in the United States (averaging over 2.11 million copies every weekday), and among English-language broadsheets, it comes second worldwide, behind only the 3.14 million daily-paid copies of *The Times of India*. USA Today is distributed in all fifty states, Canada, the District of Columbia, Puerto Rico, and Guam.

USA Today was founded in 1982 with the goal of providing a national newspaper in the U.S. market, where generally only a single local newspaper and/or a metropolitan daily's state/regional edition was available. The first issue reported on the death of actress Grace Kelly. Colorful and bold, with many large diagrams, charts, and photographs, it contrasted with the relatively colorless papers of the time such as *The Wall Street Journal* and *The New York Times*. Emphasizing its national focus, USA Today became well-known for its national polls on public sentiment. Another distinctive feature is its "Our View/Opposing View" editorial column, which features not only the paper's view on a current event, but also the view of someone (individual or group) defending the opposing view.

USA Today is known for synthesizing news down to easy-to-read-and-comprehend stories. In the main edition seen in the United States and some Canadian cities, each edition consists of four sections: News (the oft-labeled "front page" section), Money, Sports, and Life. Each section is denoted by a certain color to differentiate sections beyond lettering and is seen in a box the top-left corner of the first page, with News being blue (section A), Money with green (section B), red for Sports (section C), and purple for Life (section D). Orange is used for bonus sections (section E or above).

Part Two Warm-up Questions

1. How many Chinese dairy brands can you tell? Which is your favorite?

2. Will the news about "contaminated Sanlu milk powder" make you give up all dairy products?

3. Which do you prefer, organic food or conventional food? And Why?

Section B Texts Reading

Text A

Sixty Percent of Adults Can't Digest Milk

http://www.usatoday.com/tech/science/2009-08-30-lactose-intolerance_N.htm?poe=HFMostPopular

By Elizabeth Weise Sept.1, 2009

1 San Francisco—Got milk? If you do, take a moment to **ponder** the true **oddness** of being able to drink milk after you're a baby.

2 No other species but humans can. And most humans can't either.

3 The long lists of food allergies some people claim to have can make it seem as if they're just finicky eaters trying to rationalize likes and dislikes. Not so. Eggs, peanuts, tree nuts, fish, shellfish soy and gluten all can wreak havoc on the immune system of allergic individuals, even causing a deadly reaction called anaphylaxis.

4 But those allergic reactions are relatively rare, affecting an estimated 4% of adults.

5 Milk's different.

6 There are people who have true milk allergies that can cause deadly reactions.

But most people who have bad reactions to milk aren't actually allergic to it, in that it's not their immune system that's responding to the milk.

7   Instead, people who are lactose intolerant can't digest the main sugar—lactose—found in milk. In normal humans, the enzyme that does so—lactase—stops being produced when the person is between two and five years old. The undigested sugars end up in the colon, where they begin to ferment, producing gas that can cause cramping, bloating, nausea, flatulence and diarrhea.

8   If you're American or European it's hard to realize this, but being able to digest milk as an adult is one weird genetic adaptation.

9   It's not normal. Somewhat less than 40% of people in the world retain the ability to digest lactose after childhood. The numbers are often given as close to 0% of Native Americans, 5% of Asians, 25% of African and Caribbean peoples, 50% of Mediterranean peoples and 90% of northern Europeans. Sweden has one of the world's highest percentages of lactase tolerant people.

10   Being able to digest milk is so strange that scientists say we shouldn't really call lactose intolerance a disease, because that presumes it's abnormal. Instead, they call it lactase persistence, indicating what's really weird is the ability to continue to drink milk.

11   There's been a lot of research over the past decade looking at the genetic mutation that allows this subset of humanity to stay milk drinkers into adulthood.

12   A long-held theory was that the mutation showed up first in Northern Europe, where people got less vitamin D from the sun and therefore did better if they could also get the crucial hormone (it's not really a vitamin at all) from milk.

13   But now a group at University College London has shown that the mutation actually appeared about 7,500 years ago in dairy farmers who lived in a region between the central Balkans and central Europe, in what was known as the Funnel Beaker culture.

14   The paper was published this week in *PLoS Computational Biology*.

15   The researchers used a computer to model the spread of lactase persistence, dairy farming, other food gathering practices and genes in Europe.

16   Today, the highest proportion of people with lactase persistence live in Northwest Europe, especially the Netherlands, Ireland and Scandinavia. But the computer

model suggests that dairy farmers carrying this gene variant probably originated in central Europe and then spread more widely and rapidly than non-dairying groups.

17　　Author Mark Thomas of University College London's dept of Genetics, Evolution and Environment says: "In Europe, a single genetic change ... is strongly associated with lactase persistence and appears to have given people with it a big survival advantage."

18　　The European mutation is different from several lactase persistence genes associated with small populations of African peoples who historically have been cattle herders.

19　　Researchers at the University of Maryland identified one such mutation among Nilo-Saharan-speaking peoples in Kenya and Tanzania. That mutation seems to have arisen between 2,700 to 6,800 years ago. Two other mutations have been found among the Beja people of northeastern Sudan and tribes of the same language family in northern Kenya.

Text B

The Real Value of Organic Food

http://food.theatlantic.com/sustainability/the-real-value-of-organic-food.php
by James McWilliams　Aug.18, 2009

1　　A few weeks ago the UK's Food Standards Agency published a report concluding that organic food was no healthier than conventionally produced food. Advocates of organic food erupted in charges of gross scientific misconduct: The FSA cherry-picked the data. It didn't take into account the impact of synthetic fertilizer and insecticides. It failed to consider the growing evidence on the connection between pesticide exposure and Parkinson's Disease. Many factors, all agreed, still had to be measured and compared.

2   These objections were sound. Still, as I watched the organic defense unfold, I experienced a grim sense of *déjà vu*. If the past is any indication, those of us who follow these matters are now doomed to wade through a heap of future studies examining the relative health benefits of organic versus conventional food.

3   A similar argument played out a generation ago over the question of agricultural yields. Could organic compete with conventional when it came to output? We still have no definitive answer. Nonetheless, the din of debate continues, with advocates arguing that organic can feed the world while detractors insist it would cause mass starvation. The only clear result of all the research has been to push interested parties to the extremes.

4   Ironically, the founders of organic agriculture cared very little about yield, nutrition, or even concrete environmental outcomes. Pioneers such as Albert Howard, Rudolf Steiner, and Lady Eve Balfour embraced organic agriculture not for its quantifiable benefits but for its philosophical appeal.

5   To grow organically was, for these pioneers, to directly oppose the excesses of industrialization. A farm, these men and women argued, shouldn't be a factory. Nature, unlike an assembly line, could not be dissected into a scattering of individual pieces and rearranged to maximize productivity. Its inputs and outputs were beyond the logic of measurement. "Nature," Howard wrote, "is the best farmer." Numbers were irrelevant to such a perspective.

6   This was a heady stance to take, and it could be acted upon by buying food. The market share for organic produce has increased 20 percent a year since 1990. But the philosophical underpinnings of the organic movement have weakened. When defenders of organic agriculture start whipping out studies proving, say, that an organic tomato has 97 percent more flavonoids than a conventional one, they fall into a fatal trap.

7   The science behind the statistic might be dead on, but this kind of science—one that reduces quality to a numerical comparison—is precisely the kind of science that the movement's founders disdained. It's why they started the movement in the first place. The moment organic agriculture began to compete in the numbers game is the moment it began to lose its identity.

8   Organic may or may not produce enough food to feed the world. It may or may not produce healthier food. It may or may not save the environment. Scientists will always grapple with these questions. None of these debates really matters. What matters is that organic does one thing that no other method of food production can claim to do: it works from the premise that nature has an economy all its own, an economy that transcends facts and figures, places nature ahead of short-term profit, and operates according to a logic that cannot be quantified. For those who believe that food should be produced without strict adherence to a balance sheet, comparative studies like the FSA's will mean next to nothing. What we're talking about here is spiritual, not statistical.

Section C   After Reading

I. *Vocabulary Builder*

1. Do NOT consult the dictionary, and guess the meanings of the underlined words with the help of one or two sentences.

   The following items are for Text A:

   1) a. The storm **_wreaked havoc_** on trains and highways, making it unlikely thousands of investors and traders will arrive at work.

      b. They have **_wreaked_** dreadful **_havoc_** among the wildlife by shooting and trapping.

   2) a. The defendant is **_presumed_** innocent until proved guilty.

      b. From the way he talked, I **_presumed_** him to be your boss.

   3) a. Buddhism **_originated_** in India and came to China in the first century A.D.

      b. All theories **_originate_** from practice and in turn serve practice.

The following items are for Text B:

4) a. Taking a career history along with you will be a clear *indication* that you are well organized.

   b. There was no *indication* of forced entry to the build.

5) a. It's much easier to find the information on the Internet, rather than *wading through* piles of documents.

   b. We **waded through** a huge pile of applications, and finally selected six people to interview.

6) a. As a result of controls and the land reforms which the government carried out, agricultural *output* increased dramatically.

   b. The average *output* of the factory is 20 cars a day.

7) a. Most West European countries have *embraced* the concept of high-speed rail networks with enthusiasm.

   b. By the end of the last century, Americans had *embraced* the idea of the right to free public education for all children.

8) a. An *excess* of fat in one's diet can lead to heart disease.

   b. Drinking is OK as long as you don't do it to *excess*.

9) a. The specimens were carefully *dissected* and examined under a microscope.

   b. Surgeons of early 19th century needed dead bodies to *dissect*. This was the only way that they could learn about the flesh and bones inside the body, and the only way to teach new surgeons to carry out operations.

10) a. Organic may or may not produce enough food to feed the world. It may or may not produce healthier food. It may or may not save the environment. Scientists will always *grapple with* these questions.

    b. The government has to *grapple with* the problem of unemployment.

2. Complete the sentences using words given in the box, change forms when necessary.

adaptation	advocate	definitive	erupt
exposure	gross	retain	presume
unfold	yield		

1) Prolonged _____ to the sun can cause skin cancer.
2) If you want to _____ a copy of the original version of the letter, send a photocopy.
3) From the way he talked, I _____ him to be your boss.
4) Violence _____ after police shot a student during the demonstration.
5) An employer need not give any notice if the employee's conduct constitutes _____ misconduct justifying instant dismissal.
6) We have calculated the probable _____ from this investment at around 17%.
7) As the result of new research _____, the similarity between birdsong and our own speech behavior become more and more obvious.
8) Our company's _____ to shifting consumer tastes has been a great success.
9) Will the UK suffer a double-dip recession? No. Such a _____ answer is dangerous: we still know very little, but here are the reasons why I think the outlook for 2010 is somewhat rosier than for 2009.
10) Clinton was seen as a strong _____ for a variety of educational improvements.

II. Sentence Translation

1. The long lists of food allergies some people claim to have can make it seem as if they're just finicky eaters trying to rationalize likes and dislikes. (Para. 3, Text A)

   _____

   _____

2. Still, as I watched the organic defense unfold, I experienced a grim sense of *déjà vu*. If the past is any indication, those of us who follow these matters are now doomed to wade through a heap of future studies examining the relative health benefits of organic versus conventional food. (Para. 2, Text B)

   _____

   _____

3. When defenders of organic agriculture start whipping out studies proving, say,

that an organic tomato has 97 percent more flavonoids than a conventional one, they fall into a fatal trap. (Para. 6, Text B)

_____

_____

4. The science behind the statistic might be dead on, but this kind of science—one that reduces quality to a numerical comparison—is precisely the kind of science that the movement's founders disdained. (Para. 7, Text B)

_____

_____

5. What matters is that organic does one thing that no other method of food production can claim to do: it works from the premise that nature has an economy all its own, an economy that transcends facts and figures, places nature ahead of short-term profit, and operates according to a logic that cannot be quantified. (Para. 8, Text B)

_____

_____

III. Comprehension of the Texts

Answer the following questions.

Questions 1—6 are for Text A:

1. What is "lactose intolerance"? And why do most people suffer from it? (Paragraph 7)
2. Which race enjoys the highest milk—digesting ability in adulthood? (Paragraph 9)
3. Should "lactose intolerance" be depicted as a disease? Why or why not? (Paragraph 10)
4. Where did the milk drinker first appear according to the old theory? And why?
5. What is the new theory proposed by University College London about the origination of genetic mutation?
6. What is the discovery of the scientists at the University of Maryland?

Questions 7—9 are for Text B:

7. Why do the supporters of organic food consider the PSA's report as "scientific misconduct"?
8. There are two debates about the organic food and conventional one. What are the points of them respectively?
9. What is the psychological theory behind organic food production?

Unit 5

Crime

Section A Before Reading

Part One   Lead-in

The Economist: weekly magazine of news and opinion published in London and generally regarded as one of the world's preeminent journals of its kind. It provides wide-ranging coverage of general news and particularly of international and political developments and prospects bearing on the world's economy. It was founded in 1843 by Scotsman James Wilson as a voice against grain import tariffs. The publication maintains the position that free markets provide the best method of running economies and governments. Articles are published without bylines (there is also no masthead), thereby presenting a unified face to the publication's audience. Circulation is about 725,000, with North America accounting for about half of total readership.

The Economist's primary focus is world news, politics and business, but it also runs regular sections on science and technology as well as books and the arts. Every two weeks, the publication adds an in-depth special report on a particular issue, business sector or geographical region. Every three months, it publishes a technology report called Technology Quarterly or TQ.

The publication's writers adopt a tight style that seeks to include the maximum amount of information in a limited space. The editorial staff enforces a uniform voice throughout its pages, as if most articles were written by a single author, displaying dry, understated wit, and precise use of language. Articles involving economics do not presume any formal training on the part of the reader and aim to be accessible to the educated layperson. The newspaper usually does not translate short French quotes or phrases, and sentences in Ancient Greek or Latin are not uncommon. It does, however, describe the business or nature of even well-known entities, for example, "Goldman Sachs, an investment bank."

Part Two Warm-up Questions

1. What will you do if you witness a thief is pocket-picking a stranger to you on the street?

2. Will you give the 100,000 worth of cash you just take from the bank to an armed robber?

3. What can we do to fight crime as a college student?

Section B Texts Reading

Text A

Despite DNA Evidence, Twins Charged in Heist Go Free

http://www.time.com/time/world/article/0,8599,1887111,00.html

By Claudia Himmelreich / Berlin   Mar. 23, 2009

A police officer on a motorbike drives past the main entrance to Berlin's iconic Kaufhaus des Westens department store

1   It's an idea beloved of screenwriters: the perfect crime. But in Hollywood movies even the cleverest plot is usually derailed by an unforeseen hitch. Now a real-life heist in Germany seems to have flouted that rule together with its moral-laden subtext

that crime doesn't pay. In January 5,000,000 ($6,800,000) worth of jewelry was grabbed from the cases of Kaufhaus des Westens, a luxurious seven-story department store universally known as KaDeWe and as much of a Berlin landmark as the Victory Column and the Brandenburg Gate. Three masked, gloved thieves were caught on surveillance cameras sliding down ropes from store skylights, outsmarting the department store's sophisticated security system.

2   That night they got clean away, but they did leave evidence: DNA, found in a drop of sweat on a latex glove discarded next to a rope ladder used to reach the ground floor. Police ran the material through the German crime database. And they got a hit—two in fact.

3   The computer identified 27-year old identical twins Hassan and Abbas O. (under German law they cannot be named in full). The unemployed and Lebanese-born brothers have lived in the northern German state of Lower Saxony since age 1 but still have not been granted permanent residency. They have criminal records for theft and fraud.

4   Police arrested them on Feb. 11 in a gambling arcade and charged both brothers with burglary, an offense which carries a potential 10-year-sentence. But, on March 18, before the case ever came to trial, they were released. The twins—who have made no comment on the charges—"are laughing at the rule of law in this country," opined Germany's mass-market daily newspaper *Bild*.

5   Here's the joke: the authorities had no choice as the court ruling made clear: "From the evidence we have, we can deduce that at least one of the brothers took part in the crime, but it has not been possible to determine which one." Identical twins share 99.99% of their genetic information, and the tiny differences are impossible to isolate due to their nature—they tend to be spontaneous mutations limited to certain organs or tissues. "Identifying those [differences] would amount to dissecting the suspects," says Professor Peter M. Schneider, a University of Cologne forensic expert. "Our hands are tied in a case like this", says criminal law expert Professor Hans-Ullrich Paeffgen of Bonn University. "The law doesn't allow us to detain someone indefinitely just because he is suspected of a crime. This may be different elsewhere. But I'd rather live in a country where someone guilty is not convicted for lack of conclusive evidence than in a place where innocent people are locked up."

6   This isn't the first time identical twins have proved impossible to pin down. Their genetic material can thwart paternity tests if both twins claim—or deny—fathering a child. A jury in a rape trial in Houston deadlocked in 2005 when the DNA recovered on the crime scene matched identical twins who had kidnapped their victim together. A year earlier in Boston, a suspected rapist, an identical twin, blamed his brother when confronted with the matching DNA. Although he was already serving a sentence following a rape conviction, the jury could not agree on a verdict and the judge declared a mistrial. Earlier this year, an identical twin suspected of drug smuggling and sentenced to death in Malaysia was set free when the court could not prove beyond doubt whether he or his brother had committed the crime.

7   If fresh evidence emerges, a new arrest warrant can be issued against Hassan and Abbas O. any time within the next 10 years, the statute of limitation for burglary cases. Police will continue to keep an eye on them, hoping to be led to the loot. But with the brothers' arrest warrants suspended, they are free to travel and the authorities cannot tap their phone lines or keep tabs on their bank accounts.

8   "The mills of justice grind slowly, and sometimes not very finely," says Prof. Paeffgen, drily. The twins disagree. "We are proud of the German legal system and grateful," they told Berlin's daily newspaper *Tagesspiegel* through a family member after their release.

Text B

Forensic science

The "CSI effect"

Television dramas that rely on forensic science to solve crimes are affecting the administration of justice

From *The Economist* Apr. 22, 2010

1   Opening a new training centre in forensic science (pictured above) at the University of Glamorgan in South Wales recently, Bernard Knight, formerly one of Britain's chief pathologists, said that because of television crime dramas, jurors today

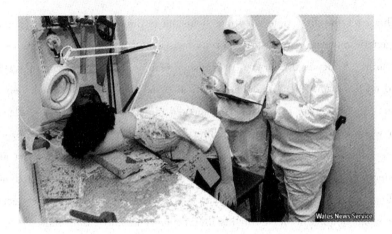

expect more categorical proof than forensic science is capable of delivering. And when it comes to the gulf between reality and fiction, Dr Knight knows what he is talking about: besides 43 years' experience of attending crime scenes, he has also written dozens of crime novels.

2   The upshot of this is that a new phrase has entered the criminological lexicon: the "CSI effect" after shows such as "CSI: Crime Scene Investigation". In 2008 Monica Robbers, an American criminologist, defined it as "the phenomenon in which jurors hold unrealistic expectations of forensic evidence and investigation techniques, and have an increased interest in the discipline of forensic science."

2   Now another American researcher has demonstrated that the "CSI effect" is indeed real. Evan Durnal of the University of Central Missouri's Criminal Justice Department has collected evidence from a number of studies to show that exposure to television drama series that focus on forensic science has altered the American legal system in complex and far-reaching ways. His conclusions have just been published in *Forensic Science International*.

4   The most obvious symptom of the CSI effect is that jurors think they have a thorough understanding of science they have seen presented on television, when they do not. Mr Durnal cites one case of jurors in a murder trial who, having noticed that a bloody coat introduced as evidence had not been tested for DNA, brought this fact to the judge's attention. Since the defendant had admitted being present at the murder scene, such tests would have thrown no light on the identity of the true culprit. The judge observed that, thanks to television, jurors knew what DNA tests could do, but

not when it was appropriate to use them.

Cops and robbers

5   The task of keeping jurors' feet on the ground falls to lawyers and judges. In one study, carried out by Dr Robbers in 2008, 62% of defence lawyers and 69% of judges agreed that jurors had unrealistic expectations of forensic evidence. Around half of respondents in each category also felt that jury selection was taking longer than it used to, because they had to be sure that prospective jurors were not judging scientific evidence by television standards.

6   According to Mr Durnal, prosecutors in the United States are now spending much more time explaining to juries why certain kinds of evidence are not relevant. Prosecutors have even introduced a new kind of witness—a "negative evidence" witness—to explain that investigators often fail to find evidence at a crime scene.

7   Defence lawyers, too, are finding that their lives have become more complicated. On the positive side, they can benefit from jurors' misguided notion that science solves crimes, and hence that the absence of crime-solving scientific evidence constitutes a reasonable doubt and grounds for acquittal. On the other hand they also find themselves at pains to explain that one of television's fictional devices—an unequivocal match between a trace of a substance found at a crime scene and an exemplar stored in a database, whether it be fingerprints, DNA or some other kind of evidence—is indeed generally just fiction.

8   In reality, scientists do not deal in certainty but in probabilities, and the way they calculate these probabilities is complex. For example, when testifying in court, a fingerprint expert may say that there is a 90% chance of obtaining a match if the defendant left the mark, and a one in several billion chance of a match if someone else left it. In general DNA provides information of a higher quality or "individualizing potential" than other kinds of evidence, so that experts may be more confident of linking it to a specific individual. But DNA experts still deal in probabilities and not certainties. As a result of all this reality checking, trials are getting longer and more cases that might previously have resulted in quick convictions are now ending in acquittals.

9   Criminals watch television too, and there is evidence they are also changing their behaviour. Most of the techniques used in crime shows are, after all, at least

grounded in truth. Bleach, which destroys DNA, is now more likely to be used by murderers to cover their tracks. The wearing of gloves is more common, as is the taping shut—rather than the DNA-laden licking—of envelopes. Investigators comb crime scenes ever more finely for new kinds of evidence, which is creating problems with the tracking and storage of evidence, so that even as the criminals leave fewer traces of themselves behind, a backlog of cold-case evidence is building up.

10   The CSI effect can also be positive, however. In one case in Virginia jurors asked the judge if a cigarette butt had been tested for possible DNA matches to the defendant in a murder trial. It had, but the defence lawyers had failed to introduce the DNA test results as evidence. When they did, those results exonerated the defendant, who was acquitted.

11   Mr Durnal does not blame the makers of the television shows for the phenomenon, because they have never claimed their shows are completely accurate. (Forensic scientists do not usually wield guns or arrest people, for one thing, and tests that take minutes on television may take weeks to process in real life.) He argues that the CSI effect is born of a longing to believe that desirable, clever and morally unimpeachable individuals are fighting to clear the names of the innocent and put the bad guys behind bars. In that respect, unfortunately, life does not always imitate art.

Section C After Reading

I. Vocabulary Builder

1. Read through Text A and B and find the English counterparts of the following Chinese words or phrases.

   The following items are for Text A:

   1) 监视摄像头　　　　　　　　　2) 从商店天窗沿绳子滑下
   3) 被授予永久居留权　　　　　　4) 偷窃与诈骗的犯罪记录
   5) 赌博游戏厅　　　　　　　　　6) 法律专家
   7) 无限期地拘留某人　　　　　　8) 缺乏确凿证据
   9) 父亲身份鉴定　　　　　　　　10) 犯罪现场
   11) 服刑　　　　　　　　　　　　12) 毒品走私

13) 发出逮捕令　　　　　　14) 抢劫案的诉讼时效
15) 监听电话

The following items are for Text B:

16) 司法　　　　　　　　　17) 法庭科学
18) 明确的证据　　　　　　19) 怀有不切实际的期待
20) 电视连续剧　　　　　　21) 被告
22) 真凶　　　　　　　　　23) 辩护律师
24) 检控官　　　　　　　　25) 以无罪宣判告结
26) 用胶条密封的信封　　　27) 烟头
28) 道德上无可指摘的个人

2. Complete the sentences using words given in the box, change forms when necessary.

| convict | deduce | demonstrate | discipline | deadlock |
| imitate | prospective | relevant | subtext | upshot |

1) The spokesman has denied this visit has any political _____.
2) Instead of being _____ of first-degree murder, Mitchell got six years for voluntary manslaughter.
3) We can only make minor concessions, but it might break the _____.
4) Darwin's observations led him to _____ that plants and animals could adapt to their surroundings.
5) I met Ivo last year at a party, and the _____ is that we're getting married on Saturday.
6) The traditional academic _____ are becoming less popular among students who now prefer more vocational subjects such as business studies.
7) The skiing instructor started the lesson by _____ turning techniques.
8) Tonight's documentary will be highly _____ to any woman who has suffered discrimination in the workplace.
9) The most common way to approach a _____ customer is to simply pick up the phone and call her.
10) Though too many people competing to _____ Michael Jackson, but always no one can surpass him.

3. Study the following synonyms and fill in each of the blanks with one from the box, change forms when necessary.

If you want to say *the act or crime of killing someone*, you can use:

> a) **murder**: [cn., un.] *the act or crime of deliberately killing someone*
> b) **homicide**: [cn., un.] *the crime of killing someone, especially deliberately—used especially in American legal contexts*
> c) **manslaughter**: [un.] *the crime of killing someone by accident, or while you are trying to defend yourself*

1) The incidence of violent crimes—_____, rape, and assault—has increased in inner city areas.
2) She denied murdering her husband, but pleaded guilty to _____.
3) As yet no evidence has been found to suggest that this death was _____.

If you want to say 判决, you can use:

> a) **convict**: [vt.] *to prove or officially announce that someone is guilty of a crime after a trial in a law court*
> b) **verdict**: [cn.] *an official decision reached by a jury, especially about whether someone is guilty of a crime*
> c) **sentence**: [vt.] *if a judge sentences someone who is guilty of a crime, they give them a punishment*

4) Despite the videotape, a jury in Simi Valley concluded a year later that the evidence was not sufficient to _____ the officers.
5) Within hours of the jury's _____, Los Angeles erupted in riots.
6) The judge said that his was a very serious crime, and _____ him to eight years in prison.
7) All four men were _____ of illegally bringing drugs into the country.
8) There was not enough evidence for a guilty _____.

II. Sentence Translation

1. It's an idea beloved of screenwriters: the perfect crime. But in Hollywood movies

Unit 5 53
Crime

even the cleverest plot is usually derailed by an unforeseen hitch. Now a real-life heist in Germany seems to have flouted that rule together with its moral-laden subtext that crime doesn't pay. (Para. 1, Text A)

_____

2. But I'd rather live in a country where someone guilty is not convicted for lack of conclusive evidence than in a place where innocent people are locked up. (Para. 5, Text A)

_____

3. Although he was already serving a sentence following a rape conviction, the jury could not agree on a verdict and the judge declared a mistrial. (Para. 6, Text A)

_____

4. On the positive side, they can benefit from jurors' misguided notion that science solves crimes, and hence that the absence of crime-solving scientific evidence constitutes a reasonable doubt and grounds for acquittal. (Para. 7, Text B)

_____

5. On the other hand they also find themselves at pains to explain that one of television's fictional devices—an unequivocal match between a trace of a substance found at a crime scene and an exemplar stored in a database, whether it be fingerprints, DNA or some other kind of evidence—is indeed generally just fiction. (Para. 7, Text B)

_____

III. Comprehension of the Texts

Answer the following questions.

Questions 1—6 are for Text A:

1. What happened to KaDeWe department store?
2. Is there any evidence left that can help find the suspects?

3. Why were the twin brothers released even before the trial?
4. Why it is impossible to determine which one of the twin brothers committed the crime?
5. Are there any other similar twins cases?
6. Will these twin brothers in this case just run away without being punished?

Questions 7—12 are for Text B:

7. What is the definition of the criminological term "CSI effect"?
8. How many experts have proved the existence of "CSI effect"? And please name them.
9. Which is the topic sentence of Paragraph 4?
10. Why does the jury selection take a longer time than before?
11. How many news tricks do the criminals learn from the CSI-like TV series?
12. What is the root of the "CSI effect" according to Mr Durnal?

Unit 6 Disaster

Section A Before Reading

Part One   Lead-in

Natural disaster is a consequence when a natural hazard (e.g., volcanic eruption or earthquake) affects humans. Human vulnerability, caused by the lack of appropriate emergency management, leads to financial, environmental, or human impact.

Man-made disaster: Disasters caused by human action, negligence, error, or involving the failure of a system are called man-made disasters. Man-made disasters are in turn categorized as technological or sociological. Technological disasters are the results of failure of technology, such as engineering failures, transport disasters, or environmental disasters. Sociological disasters have a strong human motive, such as criminal acts, stampedes, riots and war.

Risks of hypothetical future disasters:
Desertification Drought Economic Collapse Global warming Famine
Gulf Stream shutdown Hypercane Ice Age Meteorite impact
Mass extinction Megathrust earthquake Megatsunami Nuclear warfare
Overconsumption Overfishing Overpopulation Pandemic
Peak oil Sea level rise Supervolcano Terrorism Water crisis

Part Two   Warm-up Questions

1. Many areas in China and the world suffer the drought. What contribution can you make to solve this problem on daily basis?

2. Which disaster has the most destructive power in your mind? And why?

3. What would you do if you encountered a fire at the accommodation building?

Section B Texts Reading

Text A

Drought in northern China

The Rainman Comes

Farmers pay the price for decades of wasteful water use

http://www.economist.com/world/asia/displayStory.cfm?story_id=13109976

From *The Economist* Feb. 12, 2009

1   As China's 15-day lunar new year holiday began, Wen Jiabao, China's prime minister, was in the plush Swiss resort of Davos, hobnobbing with other global powerbrokers. Towards the end of the holiday on February 8, he appeared in a very different setting. Sporting a pair of smart white trainers, he strode through a grain field in the village of Yangbei, Henan province. He squatted down to talk to local farmers to offer them help to see them through a severe drought that now plagues Henan and six other provinces in northern and central China.

2   After 100 days without precipitation in the region, the government has declared

a "Level 1" emergency for the worst drought in 50 years, authorising an extra 300m yuan ($44m) in special drought-relief spending. It will finance everything from cloud-seeding rockets to the digging of new wells and tankers to deliver water. This year's winter-wheat harvest is at risk. February 8 saw some rain, but only 5—10 millimetres, compared with 200mm farmers say they need in coming months.

3   The drought comes at a difficult moment. The global downturn has hit China's exporters hard, and millions of rural migrants have lost their jobs in coastal factories and returned to their villages. Mr Wen pleased local farmers with what he had to say. They have already received help from the government, which last year invested in a new deep well. Like many of her neighbours, Fang Yue-ling, a farmer, was confident such high-profile promises would presage more assistance.

4   About 250km (150 miles) to the north, in neighbouring Shanxi province, in Pingdong, a much poorer village, 250 people live along battered dirt roads, and try to grow wheat, corn, soyabeans and winter melon on the dry, rocky mountain land. There, Guo Yongxin says he knows nothing of the government's drought-relief campaign. "We rely on the heavens for our water and we know it won't come to us from any place else." He says Pingdong is lucky because, unlike some other places, at least it has enough water for drinking and daily life. But this year, it is not enough for farming. He reckons his harvest this year will at best be half of last year's.

5   Such water scarcity is nothing new for this part of China, and neither is government attention to the issue. The region is home to the Red Flag Canal, a massive water project. According to the official tale told at the elaborate commemorative museum near Linzhou, workers, using little more than hand-tools, took all of the 1960s to build the 1,500km waterway and its 462 reservoirs and ponds. The "Red Flag Canal Spirit" has ever since been held up as a shining example of self-reliance, socialist solidarity and selfless devotion.

6   As population and living standards rise, such virtues will not be enough. China's water woes will only worsen, especially for farmers. When supplies tighten, urban and industrial users usually have priority. Ma Jun, a water specialist in Beijing, says that since the 1950s China has been digging ever deeper wells, and building ever more dams, canals, and water diversion projects. But all this has taken a

toll. Because of lower water-tables and depleted aquifers, many rivers can no longer replenish themselves in the dry season. The government's current emergency measures are necessary in the short term. But he argues that in the long term the focus must shift to conservation, efficiency, and more rational pricing so that city users pay their fair share. He concedes the Red Flag Canal is a "genuine miracle" and that there is a role for other grand projects. But, looking ahead, he argues that, in China's ability to go on tampering with its natural-water resources, "we have reached our limit."

Text B

How to Survive A Disaster

http://www.time.com/time/magazine/article/0,9171,1810315,00.html
By Amanda Ripley   May 29, 2008

1 The recent earthquake in China and the cyclone in Burma, not to mention the battery of tornadoes and wildfires ripping through the U.S. this season, remind us that disasters are part of the human condition. We are more or less vulnerable to them, depending where we live.

2 But we can do far more than we think to improve our odds of preventing and surviving even the most horrendous of catastrophes. It's a matter of preparation—bolting down your water heater before an earthquake or actually reading the in-flight safety card before takeoff—but also of mental conditioning. Each of us has what I call a "disaster personality," a state of being that takes over in a crisis. We can refine that personality and teach our brains to work more quickly, maybe even more wisely.

3 We could, for example, become far better at judging threats before catastrophe strikes. We have technological advantages that our ancestors lacked, and we know where disasters are likely to occur. And yet we flirt shamelessly with risk. We construct city skylines in hurricane alleys and neighborhoods on top of fault lines—as if nature will be cowed by our audacity and leave us be. And we rely on a sprawling

network of faraway suppliers for necessities like warmth and food. If the power cuts off, many of us still don't know where the stairs are in our skyscrapers, and we would have trouble surviving for a week without Wal-Mart. Hurricane season starts June 1, and forecasters predict a worse-than-average summer. But for many of us, preparation means little more than crossing our fingers and hoping to live.

4 Over the years, I have interviewed survivors of unimaginable tragedies. Most say that during their ordeals, almost nothing felt, sounded or looked the way they would have expected. Reality was in some ways better, in other ways worse. They say there are things they wish they had known, things they want you to know. Here, then, are three of their stories, accompanied by some of the hard wisdom of loss and luck:

Panic Can Be Your Friend

5 When disaster strikes, a troubling human response can inflate the death toll: people freeze up. They shut down, becoming suddenly limp and still. That's what happened to some people on Sept. 28, 1994, when the M. V. Estonia went down in the Baltic Sea, the worst sea disaster in modern European history.

6 Kent Härstedt, now a member of Sweden's Parliament, was then a 29-year-old passenger. That night he was hanging out in one of the ship's bars, with about 50 other passengers. "There was karaoke music," he recalls. "Everybody was laughing and singing." But just after 1 a. m., the Estonia suddenly listed starboard 30°, hurling passengers, vending machines and flowerpots across its passageways. In the bar, almost everyone fell violently against the side of the boat. Härstedt managed to grab on to the iron bar railing and hold on, hanging above everyone else.

7 "In just one second, everything went from a loud, happy, wonderful moment to total silence. Every brain, I guess, was working like a computer trying to realize what had happened," he says. Then came the screaming and crying. People had been badly hurt in the fall, and the tilt of the ship made it extremely difficult to move.

8 Contrary to popular expectations, this is what happens in many disasters. Crowds generally become quiet and docile. Panic is rare. The bigger problem is that

people do too little, too slowly. They sometimes shut down completely, falling into a stupor.

9 Firefighters, police trainers—even stockbrokers—have told me similar stories of seeing people freeze under extreme stress. But the more encouraging point is that the brain is plastic. It can be trained to respond more appropriately. Fire drills, particularly if they are mandatory and unexpected, can dramatically reduce fear, should the worst come to pass. Just knowing where the stairs are gives your brain an advantage. Likewise, research into plane crashes has found that people who read the safety briefing cards are more likely to survive. These rituals that we consider an utter waste of time actually give our brains blueprints in the unlikely event that we need them.

We All Have Our Role to Play

10 Even in the most chaotic moments, our social relationships remain largely intact. That cohesion can have positive and negative consequences, but it helps to know what to expect.

11 On May 28, 1977, one of the deadliest fires in the U.S. broke out at a place called the Beverly Hills Supper Club, a labyrinth of dining rooms, ballrooms, fountains and gardens located on a bluff 5 miles (8 km) south of Cincinnati. There were nearly 3,000 people packed into the sprawling club on that Saturday night. All told, the fire would kill 167 of them.

12 The disaster delivered many brutal lessons. Some were obvious—and tragic: the club had no sprinkler or audible fire-alarm systems. But the fire also complicated official expectations for crowd behavior: in the middle of a crisis, the basic tenets of civilization actually hold. People move in groups whenever possible. They tend to look out for one another, and they maintain hierarchies. "People die the same way they live," says disaster sociologist Lee Clarke, "with friends, loved ones and colleagues, in communities."

13 As the smoke intensified, Wayne Dammert, a banquet captain at the club, stumbled into a hallway jammed with a hundred guests. The lights flickered off and on, and the smoke started to get heavy. But what he remembers most about that crowded hallway is the silence. "Man, there wasn't a sound in there. Not a scream,

nothing," he says. Standing there in the dark, the crowd was waiting to be led.

14   The Beverly Hills employees had received no emergency training, but they performed magnificently. The exits were few and hard to find, but Dammert directed the crowd out through a service hallway into the kitchen. "My thought was that I'm responsible for these people," he says. "I think most of the employees felt that way." McCollister, still in her wedding dress, ushered her guests outside. "I was pushing people out the door, kind of like cattle, to show them where to go," she recalls. She felt responsible: "This is my party. They were there because of me."

15   Norris Johnson and William Feinberg, then sociology professors at the University of Cincinnati, managed to get access to the police interviews with hundreds of survivors—a rare and valuable database. "We were just overwhelmed with what was there," says Feinberg, now retired. People were remarkably loyal to their identities. An estimated 60% of the employees tried to help in some way—either by directing guests to safety or fighting the fire. By comparison, only 17% of the guests helped. But even among the guests, identity shaped behavior. The doctors who had been dining at the club acted as doctors, administering cpr and dressing wounds like battlefield medics. Nurses did the same thing. There was even one hospital administrator there who—naturally—began to organize the doctors and nurses.

16   The sociologists expected to see evidence of selfish behavior. But they did not. "People kept talking about the orderliness of it all," says Feinberg. "People used what they had learned in grade-school fire drills. 'Stay in line. Don't push. We'll all get out.' People were queuing up! It was just absolutely incredible."

Section C After Reading

I. Vocabulary Builder

1. Read through Text A and B and find the English counterparts of the following Chinese words or phrases.

   The following items are for Text A:

   1) 瑞士度假胜地达沃斯   2) 在种植农作物的田间大步穿行

3）蹲在地头与当地农民交谈　　4）全球经济衰退

5）高调的承诺　　6）糟糕的土路

7）抗旱活动　　8）社会主义团结

9）无私奉献　　10）水分流工程

11）降低的地下水位

The following items are for Text B：

12）使死亡人数大增　　13）卡拉 OK 音乐

14）自动售货机　　15）火警演习

16）基本的文明秩序　　17）灯光忽明忽暗

18）实施人工呼吸　　19）缝合伤口

20）访问数据库

2. Complete the sentences using words given in the box, change forms when necessary.

concede	hierarchy	intensify	mandatory	odds
overwhelm	plague	precipitation	reckon	refine
stumble	take a/one's toll	virtue	vulnerable	woe

1) Fires continued to burn elsewhere in the West in states _____ by one of the worst droughts of the century.

2) Changes in wind appear to have been more important ecologically than changes in temperature or _____.

3) We _____ that sitting in traffic jams costs us around $9 billion a year in lost output.

4) Among her many _____ are loyalty, courage, and truthfulness.

5) The image left by these events was of a company besieged by technical, legal, marketing and customer-service _____.

6) Rising unemployment has taken its inevitable _____ on the consumption market.

7) Environmentalists _____ that it will not be easy to persuade car drivers to use their vehicles less often.

8) We also need to be aware that under pressure, all of us are _____ to alco-

hol misuse and even addiction.
9) But the _____ of becoming a millionaire are good, about one in 186,046.
10) Volvo spent three years _____ the design of their new car.
11) The Council has made it _____ for all nurses to attend a refresher course every three years.
12) She worked her way up through the corporate _____ to become president.
13) The latest merger will _____ competition among international banks.
14) In her hurry she _____ and spilled the milk all over the floor.
15) But it may be difficult for some people to pretend when they are _____ with anger.

II. Sentence Translation

1. Such water scarcity is nothing new for this part of China, and neither is government attention to the issue. (Para. 5, Text A)

2. According to the official tale told at the elaborate commemorative museum near Linzhou, workers, using little more than hand-tools, took all of the 1960s to build the 1,500km waterway and its 462 reservoirs and ponds. (Para. 5, Text A)

3. But he argues that in the long term the focus must shift to conservation, efficiency, and more rational pricing so that city users pay their fair share. (Para. 6, Text A)

4. We construct city skylines in hurricane alleys and neighborhoods on top of fault lines—as if nature will be cowed by our audacity and leave us be. And we rely on a sprawling network of faraway suppliers for necessities like warmth and food.

If the power cuts off, many of us still don't know where the stairs are in our skyscrapers, and we would have trouble surviving for a week without Wal-Mart. (Para. 3, Text B)

_____

_____

5. Fire drills, particularly if they are mandatory and unexpected, can dramatically reduce fear, should the worst come to pass. (Para. 9, Text B)

_____

_____

III. Comprehension of the Texts

Answer the following questions.

Questions 1—11 are for Text A:

1. Why did Mr Wen appear in a village of Henan province?
2. What has the government done to fight the drought?
3. What will be jeopardized by the long term drought in this area?
4. Why did the drought make the situation in China turn from bad to worse?
5. What is Yangbei people's attitude toward government's drought-relief campaign?
6. What does the the people in Pingdong think of the government's drought-fighting measures?
7. Why the Red Flag Canal is mentioned in Paragraph 6?
8. What is the attitude of the author toward the "Red Flag Canal Spirit"?
9. Why will the farmers suffer most due to the water shortage?
10. What is the consequence of China's fifty-year water policy?
11. What measures should the Chinese government take in the long run according to the specialist?

Questions 12—18 are for Text B:

12. What shall we do to increase the probability of surviving from a disaster?
13. What is the general reaction of the people in a disaster?
14. Which is the topic sentence in Paragraph 9?
15. Why are people who know the number of stairs easily to survive in a fire?

16. What do we learn from the fire of Beverly Hills Supper Club?
17. What's in common between Dammert and McCollister?
18. What did the two sociology professors find through the research of the database?

Unit 7
Sports

Section A Before Reading

Part One Lead-in

NBA (The National Basketball Association) is a professional basketball league, composed of thirty teams in North America (twenty-nine in the United States and one in Canada). The NBA is one of the four major North American professional sports leagues, which include Major League Baseball (MLB), the National Football League (NFL), and the National Hockey League (NHL).

Grigori Potemkin (1739—1791) was a Russian general-field marshal, statesman, and favourite of Catherine II the Great. He is widely associated with the "Potemkin Village"—fake settlements built at the direction of Russian minister Grigory Potyomkin to fool Empress Catherine II during her visit to Crimea in 1787. According to this story, Potyomkin, who led the Crimean military campaign, had hollow facades of villages constructed along the banks of the Dnieper River in order to impress the monarch and her travel party with the value of her new conquests, thus enhancing his standing in the empress' eyes. This is the origin of the phrase **Potemkin Village**, a place where a politically generated appearance covers a less impressive underside. It also refers to something that appears elaborate and impressive but in actual fact lacks substance.

Cliffs Notes are a series of student study guides available primarily in the United States. The guides present and explain literary and other works in pamphlet form or online. Endorsers say the guides help readers understand complex works, while detractors say they let students avoid even reading them.

Part Two Warm-up Questions

1. Which aspect of Yao Ming is impressive to you most?

2. What do you think of 2008 Beijing Olympics? What makes you most proud of?

3. Is there any lesson we can learn from Beijing Olympics?

Section B Texts Reading

Text A

Semi-pro: Yao Ming Buys His Former Chinese Team

http://www.time.com/time/world/article/0,8599,1910856,00.html? iid = sphere-inline-bottom
By Hannah Beech   July 16, 2009

1 The American dream **unfolds** as a familiar tale: a poor kid works hard and grows up to be a rich, successful businessman. The Chinese dream isn't so different, except in the case of basketball star Yao Ming, it goes something like this: a poor kid is pushed into a sport he has little interest in, he brings a lackluster team in Shanghai to victory in the national championships, and he gets **drafted** by the Houston Rockets, where his offensive **prowess** earns him seven NBA All-Star awards.

Fast-forward to the present and the 7-ft. 6-in. center faces bench time because of a foot injury that some speculate could end his career. What to do but follow the Chinese dream and become a successful businessman? On July 16, Yao's agent told China's state-run media that the 28-year-old Shanghai native is buying his former Chinese basketball team, the Sharks.

2   Home-team affection notwithstanding, it's not clear whether the Sharks will be a good investment for China's richest sports star. After Yao departed for the U.S. in 2002, the Sharks went from national champions to perennial league basement dwellers. At the same time, the Chinese Basketball Association (CBA) has languished, in part because young Chinese players would prefer to watch the high-octane antics of the NBA rather than the second-rate efforts of their national league, where poor coaching and antiquated playbooks have stunted the game. It doesn't help, either, that China's best players, like Yao and the New Jersey Nets' Yi Jianlian, have fled the CBA for the klieg lights of the North American league. All in all, the CBA lost nearly $17 million last season, and the Shanghai club is among one of the most financially troubled teams in the league.

3   The Sharks are currently owned by an unlikely consortium that includes a Shanghai media group, a domestic airport operator and a state sports institute. According to China's official news agency, Xinhua, Yao is in the process of buying out shares from some major investors. No estimate has been released, however, of just how much Yao will spend on his former team, for which he started training as a young teenager.

4   The Sharks' precarious finances were thrown into further turmoil this year when a major sponsor, a fertilizer and fireproof-material conglomerate called Xiyang Group, pulled out of a contract two years early. If Yao's ownership deal does go through, as expected, it's not clear how much input Yao will have in shaping the team. Although he is a product of the state-run sports machine that still dictates much of the Sharks' athletic direction, Yao has, in the past, issued oblique criticisms of the creativity-stunting and motivation-sapping style of Chinese hoops. Even if he takes the helm as the Sharks' primary owner, spurring change within a state athletic system may be too much for this big man to handle.

Text B

The Lessons of the Beijing Olympics

http://www.time.com/time/world/article/0,8599,1835582,00.html
By Hannah Beech Aug. 24, 2008

1   Could it really be over so quickly? Ever since the International Olympic Committee awarded Beijing the Summer Games in 2001, China had lavished $44 billion on transforming the capital into a city whose time was now. Stadiums were built, entire transportation networks laid out. The areas that couldn't be prettified in time were hidden behind Olympic billboards that would have made Grigori Potemkin proud. Lest visitors think that China was somehow not sophisticated enough to merit hosting the world's premier sporting spectacle, local residents were admonished not to wear more than three contrasting hues at the same time. At a time of national glory, it just wouldn't do to have clashing colors.

2   Meanwhile, Chinese athletes—who in Beijing garnered a record 51 gold medals, 15 more than the U.S.—had selflessly trained in sports that much of the local populace hardly knew anything about before the Games. No discipline was too esoteric in the pursuit of national pride. A gold medal in women's quadruple sculls rowing? Check. Men's 50m air rifle three positions? Check. Women's 75kg weightlifting? Check.

3   But on August 24, the extravaganza for which China had been grooming itself for so long ended with a 30 ton steel centerpiece called the Memory Tower, reaching five stories that came alive with acrobats dancing along its girders representing a huge human flame. The Olympic flame may be extinguished, but the Tower, the organizers explain, represents the "holy flame which will burn and never be extinguished in people's hearts."

4   The atmosphere was far different from the giddy expectation of August 8, when the Olympics kicked off. Then, there was a sense of anxiety among the Chinese of how they would be judged by the world. During the Opening Ceremony's one-hour cultural program, the hosts eagerly gave viewers around the world a Cliffs Notes history lesson. Dear exalted foreign guests, they seemed to say, did you know we Chinese have 5,000 years of history and that we invented paper and movable type and gunpowder? Pretty cool, don't you think?

5   But as the days wore on and the number of gold medals won by China's army of athletes piled up, the approval of outsiders seemed to become less important. The Olympics became a show for the locals. It helped, too, that stringent visa regulations had limited the influx of foreign tourists. The foreign press could be annoying and Beijing residents, who were always up to date with the medal count, were slightly miffed when question arose whether several medal-winning Chinese gymnasts might be underage. Polite applause for foreign competitors occasionally degenerated into boos or, just as bad, half-empty stadiums—this despite vows that all Olympic tickets had been sold. By the end of the Closing Ceremony, it was clear: Yes, the world had been invited to watch Beijing 2008. But this was China's Games. The rest of the world was just a bystander.

6   Granted, China put on a fabulous show. But sporting events are about more than just center stage. Then, as though summoned by some kind of karmic force, the Olympics produced a parable for the Chinese. Like a one-man play on the perils of over-training and stifling national pressure, China's star hurdler Liu Xiang arrived in the Bird's Nest to run his first qualifying race—and then decided that it was all too much. The athlete who was supposed to be the face of China's Olympics turned his back to the crowds and limped off the track. After a shocked silence, the weeping

announcers on Chinese TV intoned that it was acceptable to continue idolizing Liu because he had done his best. Very quickly, however, gold-medal fever returned, with by-the-minute updates on just how many victories the host nation had tallied.

7   The Chinese were obsessed with medals. At the Closing Ceremony, as the athletes flowed into the stadium, the medalists were ushered in first. It was a situation at odds with the egalitarian, celebratory mood but very much in line with a results-obsessed nation whose mission was to impress and, by impressing, to dominate. The athletes, unused to being distinguished from their teammates, appeared to be flummoxed, unsure of how to occupy the vast amount of space in the center of the Bird's Nest. Even during the pop interludes, the athletic participants were subdued, choosing to stand or sit rather than dance.

8   The Games are moving on. And Britain, which scored its best medal haul in a century, is a counterpoint to China. London has far less to prove than Beijing. It may have plenty of troubles: a congested city center, topsy-turvy real-estate prices. But lack of confidence is not one of London's problems. The Closing Ceremony's eight-minute preview spot for the upcoming host featured a charming double-decker bus loaded with a small cast of characters that included rocker Jimmy Page. The organizers of London 2012 said they didn't want to compete with the Closing Ceremony's cast of thousands—7,000 performers, in fact, on top of the 15,000 used in the Opening Ceremony—employed by Chinese director Zhang Yimou, who was in charge of both ceremonies. But small can delight, too.

9   Perhaps, looking back on Beijing 2008, we will judge the Games as the moment that China assumed the role of future superpower. Tokyo '64 was like that, heralding the emergence of what was to become the world's second-largest economy. Or, maybe, like Berlin '36, the Olympics will shine a light on a repressive, closed political system. The enduring legacy of Beijing 2008 won't be known for some time. For now, we can celebrate the accomplishments of swift Jamaicans and amphibious Americans and, most of all, a battalion of Chinese athletes who resoundingly displaced the U.S. atop the gold-medal count. These really were China's Olympics.

With reporting by Alice Park/Beijing

Section C After Reading

I. Vocabulary Builder

1. Read through Text A and B and find the English counterparts of the following Chinese words or phrases.

   The following items are for Text A:
   1) 全国锦标赛   2) 高超的进攻能力
   3) 经纪人   4) 国营媒体
   5) 上海人   6) 国内联赛队伍
   7) 陈旧的战术指导   8) 国内机场经营者
   9) 发表间接的批评

   The following items are for Text B:
   10) 体育盛事   11) 相冲突的颜色
   12) 女子四人划艇   13) 活字印刷
   14) 外来人的赞同   15) 资格赛
   16) 宿命的力量/天意   17) 主办国
   18) 过度重视结果的   19) 持久的遗产

2. Complete the sentences using words given in the box, change forms when necessary.

degenerate	dictate	draft	languish
lest	merit	notwithstanding	peril
pursuit	spurred	stunt	turmoil
unfold			

   1) The results have been encouraging enough to _____ further investigation.

   2) The receipt had been folded and _____ so many times that it was almost in pieces.

   3) Language difficulties _____, he soon grew to love the country and its people.

4) The housing market continues to _____ due to the recession.
5) Ballou _____ a proposal which was later presented to the school board.
6) None of us who set off on that calm September morning could have foreseen the _____ that lay ahead.
7) He shivered, his thoughts in _____, his pulse racing.
8) Islamic custom _____ that women should be fully covered.
9) The growth of tourism has _____ equivalent developments in the hotel and leisure-related sectors.
10) _____ anyone should think it strange, let me assure you that it is quite true.
11) When denied, it can undermine any or all of the measures an organization has taken in _____ of healthy change.
12) A terrestrial plant will always be _____ in growth and assimilation and can never be a match for a true aquatic plant.
13) Don't allow your comments to _____ into a personal attack on the employee.

II. Sentence Translation

1. Fast-forward to the present and the 7-ft. 6-in. center faces bench time because of a foot injury that some speculate could end his career. (Para. 1, Text A)

   _____

   _____

2. No estimate has been released, however, of just how much Yao will spend on his former team, for which he started training as a young teenager. (Para. 3, Text A)

   _____

   _____

3. Although he is a product of the state-run sports machine that still dictates much of the Sharks' athletic direction, Yao has, in the past, issued oblique criticisms of the creativity-stunting and motivation-sapping style of Chinese hoops. (Para. 4, Text A)

4. Like a one-man play on the perils of over-training and stifling national pressure, China's star hurdler Liu Xiang arrived in the Bird's Nest to run his first qualifying race—and then decided that it was all too much. The athlete who was supposed to be the face of China's Olympics turned his back to the crowds and limped off the track. (Para. 6, Text B)

5. It was a situation at odds with the egalitarian, celebratory mood but very much in line with a results-obsessed nation whose mission was to impress and, by impressing, to dominate. (Para. 7, Text B)

III. Comprehension of the Texts

Answer the following questions.

Questions 1—5 are for Text A:

1. Why did Yao Ming take over the Sharks according to the author?
2. Why is it not definite that Yao Ming's purchase is a wise move?
3. What are the factors that prevent CBA from developing?
4. Who are the present owners of the Sharks?
5. What is the attitude the author hold toward Yao Ming's investment? And why?

Questions 6—14 are for Text B:

6. What preparations does China government make to guarantee successful Summer Games?
7. Which kind of attitude is held by the author toward China government's preparation?
8. What is the purpose of the construction of Memory Tower?
9. What is the mood of Chinese people on August 8 according to the author?
10. What is the author's attitude we can infer from his description of the Opening

Ceremony?

11. What makes the author deduce that the Beijing Olympics was China's Game rather than the world's?
12. What was the Chinese athletes' performance at the Closing Ceremony?
13. What does the author think of the London's eight-minute preview?
14. Why have Tokyo '64 and Berlin '36 Olympics been mentioned in Paragraph 9?

Unit 8

Art

Section A Before Reading

Part One   Lead-in

*T*he Financial Times (*FT*) is a British international business newspaper. It is a morning daily newspaper published in London. Its primary rival is New York City-based *The Wall Street Journal*.

Founded in 1888 by James Sheridan and his brother, the *Financial Times* specialises in business and financial news. Printed as a broadsheet on light salmon paper, the *FT* is the only paper in the UK providing full daily reports on the London Stock Exchange and world markets. The *FT* is usually in two sections, the first section covers national and international news, the second company and markets news.

*T*he Guardian (until 1959, *The Manchester Guardian*) is a British daily newspaper owned by the Guardian Media Group. Founded in 1821, it is unique among major British newspapers in being owned by a foundation (the Scott Trust, via the Guardian Media Group).

*T*he Guardian Weekly, which circulates worldwide, provides a compact digest of four newspapers. It contains articles from *The Guardian* and its Sunday, sister paper *The Observer*, as well as reports, features and book reviews from *The Washington Post* and articles translated from *Le Monde*.

The *Guardian* had a certified average daily circulation of 358,844 copies in January 2009—a drop of 5.17% on January 2008, as compared to sales of 842,912 for *The Daily Telegraph*, 617,483 for *The Times*, and 215,504 for *The Independent*.

Part Two Warm-up Questions

1. If you were asked to learn to play a musical instrument now, what would you choose to play? And why?

2. Do you agree that a child should be forced to learn to play a musical instrument? Why?

3. What do you think of graffiti? Is it a form of art or a destruction of city appearance? Why?

Section B Texts Reading

Text A

With Strings Attached

http://www.ft.com/cms/s/2/ad173e10-a6be-11db-83e4-0000779e2340.html
By Barbara Koh   Jan. 19, 2007

1   Away from the rumble of Shanghai's highways and the cacophony of the shopping districts, stroll down side streets filled with rows of tall brick houses. In the early evening or on a weekend morning, you'll hear the sound of classical music drifting from a piano, played by a 10-year old or a grandmother in her seventies. Wander down another alley toward drab high-rises and you'll hear Beethoven or Mozart flowing from a violin, or perhaps a cello, accordion or flute.

2   In China, classical music is booming as mightily as the 1812 Overture. It's fortissimo in Shanghai, home to China's oldest orchestra, forte in Beijing and other lively cities, and on a crescendo in farther-flung areas. Commanding Y100—200 ($12.50—$25) per hour, private music teachers in Shanghai can readily earn more than five times the average per capita monthly income.

3   Yamaha, which runs music schools in dozens of countries, opened its first in China barely a year ago. The Shanghai school already boasts 640 students. About

20,000 amateurs tackle the annual Shanghai Musicians' Association's piano proficiency exam. In addition to performances by three leading resident orchestras, Shanghai's classical calendar is supplemented with the likes of the Shanghai Sinfonietta and the Shanghai International Piano Competition. Beijing's 120-musician China Philharmonic Orchestra, founded in 2000, won ovations on its 2005 international tour, with one London reviewer trumpeting: "China has become a classical music force to be reckoned with."

4   China's classical music renaissance is a product of its roaring economy. In order to project an ultra-modern culture to match their economic success, Chinese cities have been erecting extravagant 1,000—and 2,000-seat theatres, designed by renowned architects such as Frenchman Paul Andreu, London-based Zaha Hadid and the Bastille Opera creator Carlos Ott. Meanwhile, upwardly mobile families are investing heavily in their children's cultural development.

5   "Once people have enough to eat and to wear, they need to improve their minds and souls," says Zhao Zengmao, director of the Shanghai Conservatory of Music's social education division. "Advanced countries all recognise that the arts are important." Wei Chongde, founder of the Shanghai Fugim Violin Company, had his teenage son begin piano at age five, and cello two years later. "I want to cultivate [him] to be patrician," says Wei. "If you go to a concert and can't understand it"—you applaud at the wrong time, or don't know how to talk about the music afterward—"it's embarrassing." Wei's son owns most of Yo-Yo Ma's CDs, practises at least an hour every day and takes weekly lessons with the Shanghai Symphony Orchestra's first cellist.

6   Aside from self-improvement, there are pragmatic reasons to jump on the classical bandwagon. Yo-Yo Ma, along with Deutsche Grammophon's two young piano sensations Lang Lang (who at 17 played with the Chicago Symphony Orchestra as a last-minute substitute for Andre Watts) and Li Yundi (at 18, the youngest winner in the 80-year history of the international Frederick Chopin piano competition) are worshipped like rock stars. Parents imagine their children playing their way to similar riches. Short of that, musically skilled kids get bonus points in the pressure-cooker competition to get into good universities and high schools.

7   Chinese parents also want their offspring to enjoy what they themselves could not. During the Cultural Revolution, classical music was banned. The Shanghai Conservatory, China's oldest, was considered a "cradle of western music" and so "suffered the worst", recalls its vice president, Hua Tianreng. "Half of our deans committed suicide," he says. Ironically, musicians needed to perform the eight politically correct operas approved by Mao's wife could escape the typical fate of manual labour in the countryside, so families desperately sought music teachers for their children—but couldn't afford the instruments. "The Chinese didn't have any way to learn or perform classical music," Hua says.

8   Now, of course, they can do both. And they indulge: not only in Chopin, Lizst and modern composers such as Tan Dun or Charles Ives, but also in rap, jazz, funk, blues and Chinese traditional forms. Homegrown classical ensembles and string quartets proliferate. Yet tickets to hear well-known classical musicians in the modern, grand theatres can be prohibitively expensive; most classical music fans have to make do with listening to CDs at home.

9   In mountainous, rice-growing Guangxi, Peng Yingxue began piano lessons when she was four. She caught the ear of a Shanghai Conservatory teacher who visited her kindergarten; at nine, she entered the conservatory (which accepts only 18 per cent of applicants). Her father quit his clerical job and moved to Shanghai to look after her; her mother, an office assistant, sends money from home. Peng, 15, recognises that her parents have made this sacrifice for the sake of her future. "Some people think girls are only suitable for ordinary jobs, such as being secretaries," she says. "A special skill provides you with better prospects, money and livelihood, and more choices."

10 The piano is the instrument of choice in China's classical boom. In 2002, about 600 amateur pianists took the Shanghai Conservatory's assessment exam; this year, the number was 8,000—perhaps because a piano requires slightly less dexterity and physical development than, say, a violin or clarinet. Zhao says that even senior citizens can pick it up—and about 10,000 in Shanghai have, many inspired by their grandchildren. Concert pianist Shen Wenyu, 19, adds that the newly rich may favour pianos because they "look classier and more prestigious" than other in-

struments. Many families say they chose the piano simply because everyone else did.

11   China produces more pianos and violins than anywhere else in the world: each year, about 370,000 pianos and about 2.5 million violins. In 2005, it exported about $883m-worth of instruments, the bulk of which was to the US, Japan, Germany and the UK. Simultaneously, renowned instrument makers such as Steinway & Sons have boosted their China operations. In developed countries such as Japan, up to a quarter of households own pianos. At the moment, just under 5 per cent of Shanghai households do, so piano companies are rhapsodic about China's potential.

12   Although Chinese music students are surrounded by hip contemporary music of all types, many claim to prefer the classics. "I like classical better, although it's more difficult," says Peng, a Debussy and Ravel fan. "It's been around for hundreds of years, and people still like it." Classical music's strength is its "established set of standards," says Hua. "We don't play it differently from people in Italy or Germany."

13   Despite the fervour for classical music, it gets little play in regular classrooms. "Music isn't stressed in [China's] exam-oriented education ... and in high school, music education doesn't even exist," notes Hua, who says developing lifelong classical music lovers is more important than identifying China's next classical mega-performers. He and other Chinese scholars downplay Li Yundi's and Lang Lang's stardom. They're "not Mozarts", Hua says. "We have a batch of students [graduating] every year near their level." But he's upbeat about the fate of China's classical musicians, whether or not they score Deutsche Grammophon contracts. "Our students have a very bright future, because of the good economic growth," Hua says. "They'll be in demand."

Text B

Bristol Public Given Right to Decide Whether Graffiti is Art or Eyesore

http://www.guardian.co.uk/artanddesign/2009/aug/31/graffiti-art-bristol-public-vote

by Caroline Davies Aug. 31, 2009

1   For some it is simply an eyesore, but for others graffiti has as much worth as an old master. In Bristol, reputed home of Banksy, the street artist who has done more than any other to elevate graffiti off concrete walls and into galleries, the question is to be settled by the public.

2   Bristol city council is planning to let the public vote before murals on buildings, walls and fences are scrubbed clean or painted over. If citizens decide they like it, the work will remain.

3   The move comes as the "Banksy v Bristol Museum" exhibition in the city closed today having attracted more than 300,000 visitors since June. Queues for admission were up to six hours long over the Bank Holiday weekend.

4   As part of its formal street-art policy "to seek to define and support the display of public art", the council is pledging "where people tell us that murals or artworks make a positive contribution to the local environment, and where the property owner has raised no objection" the graffiti will not be removed.

5   Photographs will be posted on the council's website and the public asked to voice their opinions.

6   The policy was created after a Banksy work, showing a naked man hanging out

of a window while his lover's partner looks for him, appeared on a council-owned building in 2005, sparking debate over whether it should be removed.

7 The council set up an online poll, with 93% of those voting saying they wanted to keep it.

8 "We have said informally that if it is street art that people like we will keep it but we want to formalise it now into a policy," said councillor Gary Hopkins, cabinet member for Environment and Community Safety.

9 "People want us to keep up the war against the taggers so we have had to work out a way to differentiate between the taggers and the artists."

10 Predictably, fine-art aficionados loathe the idea. "The two words 'graffiti' and 'art' should never be put together," said the art critic Brian Sewell. He added the council were "bonkers". "The public doesn't know good from bad."

11 "For this city to be guided by the opinion of people who don't know anything about art is lunacy. It doesn't matter if they [the public] like it. It will result in a proliferation of entirely random decoration, for want of a better word," he said.

12 "Buildings of fine quality, and there are many in Bristol, will be defaced. The architecture must take primacy over whatever street artists may want to do."

13 Bristol city council faced embarrassment in 2007 when its workers painted over a Banksy mural estimated to be worth £100,000, causing public outrage. Since then it has ordered all Banksy work to be preserved.

14 "A couple of pieces of art have been scrubbed off in error, but staff now know if it is a really good piece of art work they refer it on," said Cllr Hopkins. "Street art is part of Bristol and people have complained about Banksy in the past. But I think public opinion has shifted."

15 He said of those the Banksy exhibition has attracted, 70% were from outside the city, "so street art has generated masses of money for Bristol."

16 "Some people feel threatened by tags, so we have commissioned murals to give a positive image and that does prevent graffiti. We also get the kids that have been involved in illegal tagging and get the artist to train them."

17 The exhibition, for which the museum paid just £1 and which was free to the public, was kept secret until the day before it opened. Featuring 100 works inclu-

ding his trademark stencil paintings, animatronics and installations, organisers were forced to introduce late-night openings to keep up with visitor numbers.

18   "It has been such an amazing experience, I can't believe how great the turnout has been," said Helen Hewitt, council spokeswoman. It has seen as many visitors in its 16-week run as the museum normally attracts in a year.

19   But for Sewell, the exhibition's popularity was another sign that "the art world has gone absolutely crazy."

20   "Any fool who can put paint on canvas or turn a cardboard box into a sculpture is lauded. Banksy should have been put down at birth. It's no good as art, drawing or painting. His work has no virtue. It's merely the sheer scale of his impudence that has given him so much publicity."

Section C   After Reading

I. Vocabulary Builder

1. Do NOT consult the dictionary, and guess the meanings of the underlined words by the context, word formation, grammar, general knowledge, or any other skills you can rely on.

   The following items are for Text A:

   1) **_High-rise_** apartment buildings now stood where his childhood home had been.
   2) The new athletic center **_boasts_** an Olympic-size swimming pool.
   3) Once children have achieved a certain **_proficiency_** as a reader, they prefer to read silently.
   4) The money I get from teaching the piano is a useful **_supplement_** to my ordinary income.
   5) The **_Renaissance_** refers to the period of time in Europe between 14th and 17th centuries, when art, literature, philosophy, and scientific ideas became very important and a lot of new art was produced.
   6) Bates says he will lose his **_livelihood_** if his driving licence is taken away.
   7) When I actually visited the university, it **_inspired_** me and made me want to

go there.

The following items are for Text B:

8) They built a huge office block right next to the old cathedral—what an *eyesore*!

9) Language has *elevated* humans above the other animals.

10) My grandmother loved opera, and as she *scrubbed* the floor she would sing one aria or another.

11) The young men tried to enter a nightclub but were refused *admission*.

12) Kemp was *loathed* by all the other prisoners, who regarded him as a traitor.

13) Assisting her investigations into a perfectly natural death as if it were murder was sheer *lunacy*.

2. Complete the sentences using words given in the box, change forms when necessary.

amateur	booming	commission	cultivate	display
mighty	orchestra	outrage	proliferate	prestigious
sacrifice	spark	upbeat		

1) The need for personal protection has led to a(n) _____ private security industry here.

2) Ah, the roar of nations, they roar like the roaring of _____ waters!

3) When choosing an editor, chose a(n) _____ leader—an expert to help you create harmony from content and style.

4) Mickelson won his first major golf tournament while still a(n) _____.

5) The company has been successful in _____ a very professional image.

6) Dewey designed a new classification system for the new public libraries _____ in the UK, the USA, and elsewhere.

7) The workforce were willing to make _____ in order to preserve jobs.

8) I am a partner in one of Cleveland's oldest and most _____ law firms.

9) Analysts are more _____ about the long-term outlook for the economy.

10) They held a spectacular firework _____ to mark the new millennium.

11) Catch their interest and _____ their enthusiasm so that they begin to see

the product's potential.

12) They were _____ by the announcement of massive price increases.

13) He _____ a renowned artist to paint a picture for his wife, who is a super model.

II. Sentence Translation

1. In China, classical music is booming as mightily as the 1812 Overture. It's fortissimo in Shanghai, home to China's oldest orchestra, forte in Beijing and other lively cities, and on a crescendo in farther-flung areas. (Para. 2, Text A)

2. In order to project an ultra-modern culture to match their economic success, Chinese cities have been erecting extravagant 1,000—and 2,000-seat theatres, designed by renowned architects. Meanwhile, upwardly mobile families are investing heavily in their children's cultural development. (Para. 4, Text A)

3. Parents imagine their children playing their way to similar riches. Short of that, musically skilled kids get bonus points in the pressure-cooker competition to get into good universities and high schools. (Para. 6, Text A)

4. Yet tickets to hear well-known classical musicians in the modern, grand theatres can be prohibitively expensive; most classical music fans have to make do with listening to CDs at home. (Para. 8, Text A)

5. As part of its formal street-art policy "to seek to define and support the display of public art", the council is pledging "where people tell us that murals or artworks make a positive contribution to the local environment, and where the property owner has raised no objection" the graffiti will not be removed. (Para. 4, Text B)

III. Comprehension of the Texts

Answer the following questions.

Questions 1—4 are for Text A:

1. What is happening in China?
2. What is the root for China's classical music boom?
3. What are the incentives for China's parents to force their children to learn classic music?
4. Why most Chinese people choose to learn the piano rather than other instruments?

Questions 5—10 are for Text B:

5. Who is Banksy?
6. In Paragraph 2, there is a synonym of "graffiti". Please find it.
7. Is the "Banksy v Bristol Museum" show popular? How do you know that?
8. What triggered the formal street-art policy?
9. Why does the art critic oppose the street-art policy?
10. Why does Cllr Hopkins support the street-art policy?

Unit 9

Economy

Section A Before Reading

Part One Lead-in

2007—2008 world food price crisis: The years 2007—2008 saw dramatic increases in world food prices, creating a global crisis and causing political and economical instability and social unrest in both poor and developed nations. Initial causes of the late 2006 price spikes included unseasonable droughts in grain-producing nations and rising oil prices. Oil prices further heightened the costs of fertilizers, food transport, and industrial agriculture. These factors, coupled with falling world-food stockpiles, have all contributed to the dramatic worldwide rise in food prices. Long-term causes may include structural changes in trade and agricultural production, agricultural price supports and subsidies in developed nations, diversions of food commodities to high input foods and fuel, commodity market speculation, and climate change. As of 2009, food prices have fallen significantly from their earlier highs, although some observers believe this decrease may be temporary.

Recession 2008: Beginning in the late 2000s (December 2007 in the United States according to the National Bureau of Economic Research)—and with much greater intensity since September 2008—the industrialized world has been undergoing a recession, a pronounced deceleration of economic activity. This global recession has been taking place in a economic environment characterized by various imbalances and was sparked by the outbreak of the financial crisis of 2007—2009.

The financial crisis has been linked to reckless and unsustainable lending practices resulting from the deregulation and securitization of real estate mortgages in the United States. The financial situation was made more difficult by a sharp increase in oil and food prices. A global recession has resulted in a sharp drop in international trade, rising unemployment and slumping commodity prices. In December 2008, the National Bureau of Economic Research declared that the United States had been in recession since December 2007.

Part Two Warm-up Questions

1. Have you ever suffered from the global grain crisis?
2. What is the root of present global recession?
3. Did the 2008 financial crisis have any impact on your daily life?

Section B Texts Reading

Text A

China's grain supply

The Ravening Hoards

No need for alarm; but some Chinese ring bells anyway

http://www.economist.com/node/11058402?story_id=11058402
From *The Economist* Apr. 17, 2008

1   "With grain in our hands there is no need to panic," according to China's prime minister, Wen Jiabao. But officials worry about how to keep China near self-sufficiency in grain and sheltered from rising world prices. Mr Wen's remarks during a farm tour in Hebei in the north were meant to calm public anxieties about food-price inflation elsewhere in the world. Chinese food prices have been rising fast too in recent months, but the main impact has been on meat. Rice- and wheat-price increases have been modest, except for high-quality imports, a small share of domestic consumption. China produces more than 90% of the grain it consumes.

2   With global grain markets so jittery, officials are rather smug about having so

long stressed the need for self-sufficiency. It has enabled the government to keep the domestic market relatively calm. Early this year, to control demand, it began curbing grain exports through quotas and taxes. It promised continuing supplies to Hong Kong. But now grain importers there have had to pledge that they will not re-export. Diplomats say that China's caution has even affected the flow of food to North Korea, an old ally heavily reliant on shipments from abroad. Aid workers say North Korea is facing its worst food-supply crisis since a famine in the late 1990s.

3   Mr Wen offered reassurances that China has no shortage. When output fell in 2003, the government renewed efforts to encourage grain production (see chart). They entailed big increases in subsidies for grain farmers and in the state's guaranteed minimum purchase price for grain. Much else has also been done to raise farmers' living standards, from tax exemption to free education. This year's central-government spending on rural development including education, welfare and subsidies is due to grow by 30% to nearly $80 billion.

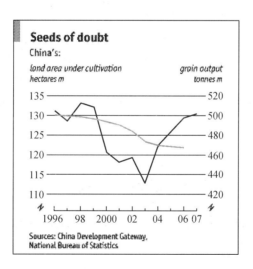

4   Last month Mr Wen even revealed what had been a state secret: that China had grain reserves of 150m—200m tonnes, equal to 30%—40% of annual production. Officials note that China's ratio of reserves to consumption is much higher than the 17%—18% level regarded by the United Nations' Food and Agriculture Organisation as a safe minimum for global stocks.

5   But not everyone is convinced. Reports in the state-controlled press say that some people in Guangdong province, next to Hong Kong, have been stockpiling grain. In March a senior agriculturalist, Yuan Longping, accused officials in some areas of exaggerating the size of grain reserves in order to get more subsidies for storing them. A commentator in the *China Daily* said export curbs would encourage smuggling. Others worry that the harsh winter in the south and spring drought in the north might dent output growth this year; and rising prices of fertiliser and other inputs could deter farmers from growing grain.

6   Officials acknowledge that maintaining near self-sufficiency in grain will become harder as the population grows and arable land shrinks. In 2006 the government said that the minimum amount of arable land needed to protect "grain security" was 120m hectares. At that time it was already giving warning that China was approaching the "red line", with about 121.8m hectares available. For local governments building on arable land is often a money-spinner. Central-government efforts to curb this have not worked. Some Chinese commentators say the line has already been crossed: some land registered as arable is in fact being used for non-agricultural purposes.

7   There has long been debate in China over whether the country's grain policy, which calls for 95% self-sufficiency, is too conservative given the potential for imports. On grain, however, conservative thinking is now back in vogue.

Text B

The Echoes of Crisis

The meltdown is real, but its impact beyond finance is still unclear

http://www.newsweek.com/id/160159
By Zachary Karabell   Sept. 29, 2008

1   "There has never been a week like this!" "There is no playbook!" "The worst financial crisis since the Great Depression!" These phrases and others of equal hyperbole were repeated any number of times on Wall Street these past weeks. No doubt the drama has been spectacular. In the space of ten days, the U.S. govern-

ment took over two mortgage-bond behemoths, Fannie Mae and Freddie Mac, and assumed de facto control of one of the world's largest insurance companies, AIG. Two of the oldest and most renowned investment banks, Lehman Brothers and Merrill Lynch, came to an end; Merrill was acquired by Bank of America for about $50 billion; and Lehman was forced into bankruptcy, with some of its more-valuable assets and employees picked up for pennies by Britain's Barclays Bank. Morgan Stanley and Goldman Sachs saw their stocks plummet and then boomerang back up. Global stock indices lost and then gained trillions in value, and central banks injected hundreds of billions to prevent the global economic system from freezing. To cap it off, the U. S. government announced a far-reaching plan to assume responsibility for the bad mortgages that triggered all this in the first place.

2 The meltdown of Wall Street and the resulting government intervention are real and will reshape the industry. But it's much less apparent what the ramifications are beyond the financial industry. The link between Main Street and Wall Street has always been mysterious. There have been Wall Street crises that barely touched the broader economy (think the Panic of 1907 and the implosion of Long Term Capital Management in 1998), and there have been Main Street downturns that have only marginally hurt Wall Street (the 1981—1982 recession). Many people say that today's crisis on Wall Street will have dire effects on the "real" economy, but for now, at least, those assertions are just that. The U. S. economy, at least as measured by GDP, has shown surprising growth through the first six months of the year, up 3.3 percent in the second quarter alone. Consumer spending has flattened but not collapsed under the weight of higher gas and food prices and tighter credit. On Main Street, there may not be much to celebrate, but it's a far cry from what's happening on Wall Street.

3 And it's not even happening everywhere on Wall Street. Trillion-dollar asset-management companies such as Fidelity and Vanguard, for instance, are doing fine, though the decline in stock prices is a negative for them. Credit-card companies like Capital One, and Visa (which had one of the most successful initial public offerings in years earlier this summer) have not seen the consumer defaults that <u>the dire rhetoric</u> would suggest. In free-fall are investment banks and anyone involved in mortga-

ges and their many derivatives, but parts of Wall Street are business as normal, though you'd never know that judging from the mood. After all, Bank of America—flush with consumer deposits from Main Street—actually had $50 billion to buy Merrill Lynch.

4 Even the absolute size of the problems isn't as dire as depicted. Investment banks and insurers like AIG have trillions of dollars in outstanding assets, obligations, and contracts. But that doesn't mean trillions of dollars in losses. Only a portion of their business is tied up with mortgages and derivatives, and while some of those might be worthless, most aren't. We know that because even in a terrible, dysfunctional market, they have been purchased.

5 The derivatives built around mortgages ultimately rest on underlying assets, namely homes. Even as those homes decline in value—whether in the United States, or the U.K., or Spain—they are still worth something. Most home price decreases are in the range of 10 percent to 20 percent, and most mortgages are not in default.

6 Swift government action also separates the current financial implosion from Great Depression-like meltdowns. The U.S. government spent a trillion dollars on Iraq in the past five years—though that money will never yield a penny. With the U.S. economy generating $14 trillion every year, the government is more than able to provide a several hundred billion dollar backstop to bad mortgages, if that proves necessary to halt the rippling panic on Wall Street or contain the next bank failure.

7 The conventional wisdom is that Wall Street is the center of the global financial system, the axis around which all revolves, and if it breaks, if the current government bailout fails to stem the bleeding, the entire world is imperiled. Short-term, there's some truth in that: the world needs liquidity (cash) just as the body needs water. But the world needs a lot of things: electricity and transportation, for instance. In 2002, the global airline industry imploded in the wake of 9/11. Globally, 150,000 people lost their jobs—more than the dire projections of job losses this year on Wall Street. The U.S. government provided $15 billion in bailout funds to airlines in November 2002 alone. In 2008, faced with sharply higher fuel costs, the U.S. airline industry has already shed 22,000 jobs, and has notched tens of billions in losses. Yet the collapse of the airline industry in both 2002 and 2008 did not lead to

claims that global travel was imperiled or that the system as we know it was teetering on the brink.

8   The bottom line—there's clearly an echo-chamber problem here. The people who report on Wall Street by and large live in the same place as the people who work on Wall Street. A similar problem exists in London with the City and Fleet Street. The analysts who assess what is happening on behalf of investors are employed by the same companies that they are supposed to be analyzing objectively. The agencies that rate the bonds of companies are part of the same nexus. And of course the traders who buy and sell are intertwined as well. Expecting any of these to have perspective is a bit like asking someone in the eye of a storm what they feel about wind and rain. Rumors spread easily, and fear can get stoked to wildfire intensity in a matter of days. The 24/7 news cycle doesn't help; drama and crisis are good for ratings.

9   Finally, Wall Street is not the world. In the past five years alone, there has been a massive wealth transfer away from the United States and in both the oil-producing regions such as the Gulf and goods-producing regions such as China. While this shift may signify a relative decrease in U.S. power, it provides a cushion for the global economic system. There may not be enough capital on Wall Street to float ailing investment banks. There is more than enough capital globally to do that many times over. Sovereign wealth funds already helped Citibank through some of its trouble at the end of 2007; China's SWF just took a larger stake in Morgan Stanley; and they could very well step in again if needed.

10   Dark days on Wall Street for sure, but stocks go up just as quickly as they go down. Others will continue to put money in their retirement plans and may find years from now that those investments performed spectacularly. Wall Street will consolidate, and some firms will thrive and profit having picked up solid franchises of imploding companies. And then some other crisis will occur, unexpected, and people will once again say that it's the worst they've ever seen, and life will go on.

Karabell is president of RiverTwice Research and senior adviser to Business for Social Responsibility.

Section C After Reading

I. Vocabulary Builder

1. Do NOT consult the dictionary, and guess the meanings of the underlined words by the context, word formation, grammar, general knowledge, or any other skills you can rely on.

   The following items are for Text A:

   1) The change in leadership will have a huge *impact* on government policy.
   2) Some economists predicted that many people would choose to own more *modest* homes at a small price during the downturn.
   3) a. Her movements seemed so *jittery*, with her quick and reluctant smile and shaky hands during the introductions.
      b. Investors are *jittery* due to uncertainty about interest rates.
   4) Lawson comes over as *smug* and arrogant, but in fact he's quite a decent man.
   5) The government is introducing new measures aimed at *curbing* inflation.
   6) Evidence given by convicted criminals should always be treated with the utmost *caution*.
   7) So, why are pandas *reliant* on bamboo?
   8) The leadership role *entails* taking the initiative in formulating, articulating, and implementing goals for the political system.
   9) Housing *subsidies*, food supplements, and health care will decline to levels that no longer can ease the pain.
   10) Short skirts are very much *in vogue* just now, with 80% girls wearing them on street.

   The following items are for Text B:

   11) Sixty-five percent of women start off breastfeeding—but that figure *plummets* to 40 percent in the six weeks after delivery.
   12) A drug that is *injected* reaches the brain faster than if it is smoked or sniffed.

13) Even the smallest diplomatic incident can *trigger* a major international conflict.

14) What shocked me was the parents' *apparent* lack of interest in their child.

15) a. The course that people choose to do at university can have *ramifications* for the rest of their lives.

   b. Whatever the judges decide, the legal *ramifications* of the case will be with us for many years to come.

16) a. Climate and geography are the *underlying* reasons for the region's low level of economic development.

   b. The *underlying* factor in almost all suicides is the feeling of hopelessness.

17) On Sept. 17 reports stated that tear gas was used to *halt* protests at a Mandalay high school.

18) The restaurant slowly *revolves*, giving excellent views of the city.

19) Though White House economic *projections* have proven relatively accurate the last four years, they are less conservative than congressional economic *projections*.

20) Teachers often have to deal with *tricky* situations such as interviews with angry parents.

2. Study the following synonyms and fill in each of the blanks with one from the box, change forms when necessary.

If you want to say 发誓, you can use:

> a) **swear**: [vt.] *to make a very serious promise, especially publicly or in a law court*
>
> b) **pledge**: [vt.] *to publicly or officially promise to give help, support, or money to an organization, group, or person, especially a politician*
>
> c) **vow**: *to firmly promise something, especially to yourself—used especially in literature*

1) The government has _____ £500,000 worth of aid to the drought-stricken area.

2) The witness stood up in court and _____ that she would tell the truth.

3) The couple made their _____ at St Paul's Church in Hayes.

If you want to say 补助, 津贴, you can use:

> a) **subsidy**: [cn.] money that is paid by a gov. or org. to make prices lower, reduce the cost of producing goods etc.
>
> b) **allowance**: [cn.] money that sb. receives regularly for a special reason, and that they do not earn by working
>
> c) **pension**: an amount of money that old people receive regularly from the government, their former employer, or an insurance company after paying in money over many years

4) He gets a pretty good _____ from his old firm where he worked for 30 years.

5) US farmers are having trouble coping with the reductions in agricultural _____.

6) Sales staff get a generous mileage _____ or a company car.

If you want to say 保留, 保存, you can use:

> a) **conserve**: use (resources/energy/materials/fuel/water etc.) very carefully so that you will have enough for the future
>
> b) **reserve**: order or set aside (seats, accommodation, etc.) for use by a particular person at a future time; book
>
> c) **preserve**: keep or maintain (sth) in an unchanged or perfect condition

7) I'd like to _____ a table for two.

8) Recycling helps _____ natural and often limited resources, such as wood and aluminum.

9) All the names in the book have been changed to _____ the victims' anonymity.

If you want to say 比率、比例, you can use:

> a) **proportion**: [cn., usually singular] the number or amount of something, compared with the whole number or amount that exists
> b) **rate**: [cn.] a measurement showing the number of times that something happens during a particular period or the number of examples of something within a certain period
> c) **ratio**: [cn., usually singular] a set of numbers, such as "20:1" or "5:1", that shows how much larger one quantity is than another

10) Australia's unemployment _____ rose to 6.5% in February.

11) Although the majority of offenders are men, a small _____ —about 5 percent—are women.

12) The new law is intended to reduce the _____ of road accidents caused by drunk drivers.

13) This changed the _____ of qualified to unqualified staff from 61 : 23 to 58 : 28.

II. Sentence Translation

1. But officials worry about how to keep China near self-sufficiency in grain and sheltered from rising world prices. (Para. 1, Text A)

2. Officials note that China's ratio of reserves to consumption is much higher than the 17%—18% level regarded by the United Nations' Food and Agriculture Organization as a safe minimum for global stocks. (Para. 4, Text A)

3. The meltdown of Wall Street and the resulting government intervention are real and will reshape the industry. But it's much less apparent what the ramifications are beyond the financial industry. (Para. 2, Text B)

4. In free-fall are investment banks and anyone involved in mortgages and their many derivatives, but parts of Wall Street are business as normal, though you'd never know that judging from the mood. (Para. 3, Text B)

5. Rumors spread easily, and fear can get stoked to wildfire intensity in a matter of days. The 24/7 news cycle doesn't help; drama and crisis are good for ratings. (Para. 8, Text B)

III. Comprehension of the Texts

Answer the following questions, or choose the best answer.

Questions 1—5 are for Text A:

1. Which of the following is the topic sentence in Paragraph 1?
   A. With grain in our hands there is no need to panic.
   B. But officials worry about how to keep China near self-sufficiency in grain and sheltered from rising world prices.
   C. Chinese food prices have been rising fast too in recent months, but the main impact has been on meat.
   D. China produces more than 90% of the grain it consumes.
2. What measures did the Chinese government take to stabilize the Chinese grain market according to Paragraph 2?
3. What is the general idea of Paragraph 3?
4. Why do some people doubt the grain supply in China?
5. Why is the quantity of arable land in China decending?

Questions 6—10 are for Text B:

6. Why is the downturn of this time regarded as "the worst ... since the Great Depression" by some people?
7. What about the relationship between Main Street and Wall Street?

8. How is consumer spending doing in America?
9. In Paragraph 3, there's a underlined phrase "the dire rhetoric", what does it refer to?
10. How does the author make his argument that people should not be too terrified of the present slump?

Unit 10

Ecology

Section A Before Reading

Part One   Lead-in

Ecology is the interdisciplinary scientific study of the interactions between organisms and the interactions of these organisms with their environment. Like many of the natural sciences, however, a conceptual understanding of ecology is found in the broader details of study, including:

The Kyoto Protocol is a protocol to the United Nations Framework Convention on Climate Change (UNFCCC or FCCC), aimed at combating global warming. The UNFCCC is an international environmental treaty with the goal of achieving "stabilization of greenhouse gas concentrations in the atmosphere at a level that would prevent dangerous anthropogenic interference with the climate system."

The Protocol was initially adopted on 11 December 1997 in Kyoto, Japan and entered into force on 16 February 2005. As of October 2009, 184 states have signed and ratified the protocol. The most notable non-member of the Protocol is the United States, which is a signatory of UNFCCC and was responsible for 36.1% of the 1990 emission levels.

Carbon credits are a key component of national and international attempts to mitigate the growth in concentrations of greenhouse gases (GHGs). One Carbon Credit is equal to one ton of Carbon. Carbon trading is an application of an emissions trading approach. Greenhouse gas emissions are capped and then markets are used to allocate the emissions among the group of regulated sources. The goal is to allow market mechanisms to drive industrial and commercial processes in the direction of low emissions or less "carbon intensive" approaches than those used when there is no cost to emitting carbon dioxide and other GHGs into the atmosphere. Since GHG mitigation projects generate credits, this approach can be used to finance carbon reduction schemes between trading partners and around the world.

Part Two Warm-up Questions

1. Describe the city you come from from environment perspective.
2. What can we do to protect the environment as an individual?
3. What are the endangered animals in the world?

Section B Texts Reading

Text A

Carbon markets in China

Verdant?

The first domestic purchase of carbon credits is less than it seems

http://www.economist.com/businessfinance/displayStory.cfm?story_id=14258926&source=hp-textfeature

From *The Economist* Aug. 20, 2009

1   China is the world's largest supplier of carbon credits. The country is due to generate 55% of all certified-emission reduction credits (CERs), which under the

Kyoto Protocol allow companies in developed nations to offset their emissions by buying credits from developing nations. But to date China has not been a source of demand. So when Tianping Auto Insurance, a Shanghai-based company, bought credits equivalent to 8,026 tons of emissions on the China Beijing Environment Exchange, an emissions-trading platform, earlier this month, analysts sat up. It was the first known example of a Chinese company buying credits to offset emissions.

2   If Tianping's purchase signals that domestic demand for carbon credits is growing, that should in theory help the fight against climate change. Investment in low-carbon projects, which range from installing cleaner stoves in homes to building wind farms, is what generates credits. The greater the demand for credits, the more attractive such projects become. So is a new Chinese boom, this time in carbon, now on the horizon?

3   Not quite. What Tianping bagged were voluntary, or verified, emission reductions (VERs). Voluntary credits are an increasingly popular means for companies to burnish their green credentials (although the crisis has muted demand recently). Last year over-the-counter transactions of VERs globally hit a record $397m, according to data from New Energy Finance (NEF), a research firm. Tianping bought credits from last year's Beijing Olympics, supposedly generated by commuters who opted for eco-friendly forms of transport.

4   Tianping's voluntary purchase shows that the concept of corporate social responsibility is no longer entirely foreign in China. But the idea is still in its infancy. A study by Syntao, a consultancy in Beijing, found that from January to November 2008 just 121 Chinese companies published "sustainability reports". Awareness of carbon offsets remains low. Tianping's $40,000 purchase was small by Western standards. And the credits were first auctioned in December—hardly a sign of feverish demand. Worryingly, they also appear not to have been audited by specialists in line with the highest standards for voluntary credits, says John Romankiewicz at NEF: it is hard to be sure, for example, that people really rode their bikes to work during the Olympics rather than jumping in taxis.

5   For domestic demand to take off, Chinese firms will probably have to be pushed. Setting a limit on companies' emissions beyond which they must buy offsets

is not thought to be on the cards, but hopes are growing that China will commit to some kind of non-binding target, possibly at the Copenhagen climate-change summit at the end of this year. Chinese negotiators recently gave a timetable for a peak in the country's emissions, albeit in far-off 2050. In June, China's state council said it plans to set a "carbon intensity" target, which would determine a certain level of emissions per unit of GDP. But detailed policies may not take shape until the launch of the next five-year plan, beginning in 2011. Tianping's move is still a rather solitary shoot of greenery.

Text B

The New Age of Extinction

http://www.time.com/time/specials/packages/article/0,28804,1888728_1888736,00.html#
By Bryan Walsh   Apr. 13, 2009

1   There are at least 8 million unique species of life on the planet, if not far more, and you could be forgiven for believing that all of them can be found in Andasibe. Walking through this rain forest in Madagascar is like stepping into the library of life. Sunlight seeps through the silky fringes of the Ravenea louvelii, an endangered palm found, like so much else on this African island, nowhere else. Leaf-tailed geckos cling to the trees, cloaked in green. A fat Parson's chameleon lies lazily on a branch, beady eyes scanning for dinner. But the animal I most hoped to find, I don't

see at first; I hear it, though—a sustained groan that electrifies the forest quiet. My Malagasy guide, Marie Razafindrasolo, finds the source of the sound perched on a branch. It is the black-and-white indri, largest of the lemurs—a type of small primate found only in Madagascar. The cry is known as a spacing call, a warning to other indris to keep their distance, to prevent competition for food. But there's not much risk of interlopers. The species—like many other lemurs, like many other animals in Madagascar, like so much of life on Earth—is endangered and dwindling fast.

2　　Madagascar—which separated from India 80 million to 100 million years ago before eventually settling off the southeastern coast of Africa—is in many ways an Earth apart. All that time in geographic isolation made Madagascar a Darwinian playground, its animals and plants evolving into forms utterly original. Some 90% of the island's plants and about 70% of its animals are endemic, meaning that they are found only in Madagascar. But what makes life on the island unique also makes it uniquely vulnerable. "If we lose these animals on Madagascar, they're gone forever," says Russell Mittermeier, president of the wildlife group Conservation International (CI).

3　　That loss seems likelier than ever because the animals are under threat as never before. Once lushly forested, Madagascar has seen more than 80% of its original vegetation cut down or burned since humans arrived at least 1,500 years ago, fragmenting habitats and leaving animals effectively homeless. Unchecked hunting wiped out a number of large species, and today mining, logging and energy exploration threaten those that remain. "You have an area the size of New Jersey in Madagascar that is still under forest, and all this incredible diversity is crammed into it," says Mittermeier, an American who has been traveling to the country for more than 25 years. "We're very concerned."

Price of Extinction

4　　There have been five extinction waves in the planet's history—including the Permian extinction 250 million years ago, when an estimated 70% of all terrestrial animals and 96% of all marine creatures vanished, and, most recently, the Cretaceous event 65 million years ago, which ended the reign of the dinosaurs. Though scientists have directly assessed the viability of fewer than 3% of the world's described species, the sample polling of animal populations so far suggests that we may have entered what will be the planet's sixth great extinction wave. And this time the cause isn't an errant asteroid or megavolcanoes. It's us.

5   A 2008 assessment by the International Union for Conservation of Nature found that nearly 1 in 4 mammals worldwide was at risk for extinction, including endangered species like the famous Tasmanian devil. Overfishing and acidification of the oceans are threatening marine species as diverse as the bluefin tuna and reef-forming corals. "Just about everything is going down," says Simon Stuart, head of the IUCN's species-survival commission. "And when I think about the impact of climate change, it really scares me."

6   Scary for conservationists, yes, but the question arises, Why should it matter to the rest of us? After all, nearly all the species that were ever alive in the past are gone today. Evolution demands extinction. What does the loss of a few species among millions matter?

7   For one thing, we're animals too, dependent on this planet like every other form of life. The more species living in an ecosystem, the healthier and more productive it is, which matters for us. When we pollute and deforest and make a mess of the ecological web, we're taking out mortgages on the Earth that we can't pay back—and those loans will come due. Then there are the undiscovered organisms and animals that could serve as the basis of needed medicines—as the original ingredients of aspirin were derived from the herb meadowsweet—unless we unwittingly destroy them first. "We have plenty of stories about how the loss of biodiversity creates problems for people," says Carter Roberts, WWF's president.

8   Forests razed can grow back, polluted air and water can be cleaned—but extinction is forever. So if you care about tigers and tamarins, rhinos and orangutans, if you believe Earth is more than just a home for 6.7 billion human beings and counting, then you should be scared. But fear shouldn't leave us paralyzed. Environmental groups worldwide are responding with new methods to new threats to wildlife. In hot spots like Madagascar and Brazil, conservationists are working with locals on the

ground, ensuring that the protection of endangered species is tied to the welfare of the people who live closest to them. A strategy known as avoided deforestation goes further, incentivizing environmental protection by putting a price on the carbon locked in rain forests and allowing countries to trade credits in an international market, provided that the carbon stays in the trees and is not cut or burned. And as global warming forces animals to migrate in order to escape changing climates, conservationists are looking to create protected corridors that would give the species room to roam. It's uncertain that any of this will stop the sixth extinction wave, let alone preserve the biodiversity we still enjoy, but we have no choice but to try.

Section C After Reading

I. Vocabulary Builder

1. Do NOT consult the dictionary, and guess the meanings of the underlined words by the context, word formation, grammar, general knowledge, or any other skills you can rely on.

   The following items are for Text A:
   1) Cuts in prices for milk, butter, and cheese will be *offset* by direct payments to farmers.
   2) The doctor *certified* me unfit to go to work for the next month.
   3) The US Congress is roughly *equivalent* to the British Parliament.
   4) To be sure, the on-line travel industry is still in its *infancy*, but it appears poised for explosive growth.
   5) An undeniable attraction of an *auction* is the possibility that some undervalued item may be for sale.
   6) The *timetable* said there was another train at 6:15.
   7) There was one *solitary* hotel left standing after the earthquake.

   The following items are for Text B:
   8) And this time the cause of the extinction isn't the *megavolcanoes* but our human beings.

9) The original 30 employees had ***dwindled*** to 12 due to the downturn.

10) Wild animals are at their most ***vulnerable*** when they are asleep.

11) His day was ***fragmented*** by interruptions and phone calls.

12) The youngster ***vanished*** without a trace one day and has never been found.

13) The tasks of selecting, evaluating, and rewarding are essential ***ingredients*** of a qualified manager.

14) He's twice suffered strokes and is ***paralyzed*** down one side of his body.

2. Complete the sentences using words given in the box, change forms when necessary.

be on the cards	binding	burnish	commit to
emission	fringe	incentive	mortgage
on the horizon	reign	verify	vulnerable

1) It estimates that in that time it cut its carbon dioxide _____ by more than 20 percent.

2) After two weeks of talks a solution to the dispute is _____.

3) For nearly three years President Clinton has carefully _____ his crime-fighter credentials.

4) In one significant way, it is true, the _____ of the new king marked a distinct break with the past.

5) His statement was _____ by several witnesses.

6) I was hoping for a promotion, but it doesn't seem to _____ right now.

7) The organization needs volunteers who can _____ to work four hours a week.

8) When prices are so low, farmers have little _____ to increase production.

9) The successful bidder is under a(n) _____ contract to purchase the relevant property.

10) The idea, indeed, was supported more by those on the _____ of political life than by those at the centre.

11) Anyone taking out a(n) _____ should be aware that interest rates can go up at any time.

12) The election defeat puts the party leader in a(n) _____ position.

II. Sentence Translation

1. Setting a limit on companies' emissions beyond which they must buy offsets is not thought to be on the cards, but hopes are growing that China will commit to some kind of non-binding target, possibly at the Copenhagen climate-change summit at the end of this year. (Para. 5, Text A)

2. Madagascar—which separated from India 80 million to 100 million years ago before eventually settling off the southeastern coast of Africa—is in many ways an Earth apart. (Para. 2, Text B)

3. Though scientists have directly assessed the viability of fewer than 3% of the world's described species, the sample polling of animal populations so far suggests that we may have entered what will be the planet's sixth great extinction wave. (Para. 4, Text B)

4. When we pollute and deforest and make a mess of the ecological web, we're taking out mortgages on the Earth that we can't pay back—and those loans will come due. (Para. 7, Text B)

5. A strategy known as avoided deforestation goes further, incentivizing environmental protection by putting a price on the carbon locked in rain forests and allowing countries to trade credits in an international market, provided that the carbon stays in the trees and is not cut or burned. (Para. 8, Text B)

III. Comprehension of the Texts

Answer the following questions.

Questions 1—6 are for Text A:

1. Why does Tianping Auto Insurance's purchasing VERs make analysts so surprised?
2. Why will the increasing demand for carbon credits benefit the fight against climate change?
3. What are the purpose of those companies which purchase VERs?
4. Why has Tianping's demand for credits been increasing since Beijing Olympics?
5. What is the significance of Tianping's voluntary purchase of credits?
6. Why does the author say the notion of corporate social responsibility is relatively new in China?

Questions 7—10 are for Text B:

7. How many animals are mentioned in Paragraph 1?
8. What have human beings been doing to destroy the ecology in Madagascar?
9. Why do human beings cannot afford the extinction of a few specials?
10. What are the new approaches the conservationists adopt to deal with new threats to wildlife?

Unit 11
Health

Section A Before Reading

Part One Lead-in

Articles can be divided into two main categories: news and features. Straight news stories deal with the timeliness and immediacy of breaking news, while feature articles are news stories that deal with human-interest topics or which offer the opportunity for providing more breadth or depth, context of history or other explanatory background material. An article generally insists of the headline, the lead, the body and the conclusion.

Headline
The headline is the text at the top of a newspaper article, indicating the nature of the article. The headline catches the attention of the reader and relates well to the topic. Modern headlines are typically written in an abbreviated style omitting many elements of a complete sentence but almost always including a non-copula verb.

Lead
The lead sentence captures the attention of the reader and sums up the focus of the story. The lead also establishes the subject, sets the tone and guides the reader into the article. In a news story, the introductory paragraph tells the most important facts and answers the questions: *who*, *what*, *where*, *when*, *why*, and *how*. In a feature story, the author may choose to open in any number of ways, including the following:

an anecdote
a shocking or startling statement
- a generalization
- pure information
- a description
- a quote

- a question
- a comparison

Body

- For the news story, details and elaboration are evident in the body of the news story and flow smoothly from the lead
    - Quotes are used to add interest and support to the story
    - The inverted pyramid is used with most news stories

A feature article will follow a format appropriate for its type. Structures for feature articles may include, but are not limited to:

- chronological—the article may be a narrative of some sort
- cause and effect—the reasons and results of an event or process are examined
- classification—items in an article are grouped to help aid understanding
- compare and contrast—two or more items are examined side-by-side to see their similarities and differences
- list—a simple item-by-item run-down of pieces of information
- question and answer—such as an interview with a celebrity or expert

Conclusion

One difference between a news story and a feature article is the conclusion. Endings for a hard news article occur when all of the information has been presented according to the inverted pyramid form. By contrast, the feature article needs more definite closure. The conclusions for these articles may include, but are not limited to:

- a final quote
- a descriptive scene
- a play on the title or lead
- a summary statement

Part Two   Warm-up Questions

1. How often do you work out each week? Which kind of sports will you choose?

2. Are there any friends or classmates of you get bonus scores because of their sports talents? Are they smart? Can they achieve good scores at school?

3. Which part aren't you satisfied with your body? Why?

Section B Texts Reading

Text A

Stronger, Faster, Smarter

Exercise does more than build muscles and help prevent heart disease. New science shows that it also boosts brainpower—and may offer hope in the battle against Alzheimer's

http://www.newsweek.com/id/36056
By Mary Carmichael Mar. 26, 2007

1   The stereotype of the "dumb jock" has never sounded right to Charles Hillman. A jock himself, he plays hockey four times a week, but when he isn't body-checking his opponents on the ice, he's giving his mind a comparable workout in his neuro-

science and kinesiology lab at the University of Illinois. With colleagues, he rounded up 259 Illinois third and fifth graders, measured their body-mass index and put them through classic PE routines: the "sit-and-reach," timed push-ups and sit-ups. Then he checked their physical abilities against their math and reading scores on a statewide standardized test. Sure enough, on the whole, the kids with the fittest bodies were the ones with the fittest brains, even when factors such as socioeconomic status were taken into account.

2 The idea of the "scholar-athlete" goes back to the culture of ancient Greece, in which "fitness was almost as important as learning itself," says Harvard psychiatrist John Ratey. The Greeks, he adds, were clued into "the mind-body connection." And they probably intuited a basic principle that Western researchers also figured out long ago: aerobic exercise helps the heart pump more blood to the brain, along with the rest of the body. More blood means more oxygen, and thus better-nourished brain cells. For decades, that has been the only link between athletic and mental prowess that science has been able to demonstrate with any degree of certainty.

3 Now, however, armed with brain-scanning tools and a sophisticated understanding of biochemistry, researchers are realizing that the mental effects of exercise are far more profound and complex than they once thought. The process starts in the muscles. Every time a bicep or quad contracts and releases, it sends out chemicals, including a protein called IGF-1 that travels through the bloodstream, across the blood-brain barrier and into the brain itself. There, IGF-1 takes on the role of foreman in the body's neurotransmitter factory. It issues orders to ramp up production of several chemicals, including one called brain-derived neurotrophic factor, or BDNF, which fuels almost all the activities that lead to higher thought.

4 With regular exercise, the body builds up its levels of BDNF, and the brain's nerve cells start to branch out, join together and communicate with each other in new ways. This is the process that underlies learning: every change in the junctions between brain cells signifies a new fact or skill that's been picked up and stowed away for future use. BDNF makes that process possible. Brains with more of it have a greater capacity for knowledge. On the other hand, says UCLA neuroscientist Fernando Gómez-Pinilla, a brain that's low on BDNF shuts itself off to new information.

5   Most people maintain fairly constant levels of BDNF in adulthood. But as they age, their individual neurons slowly start to die off. Until the mid-'90s, scientists thought the loss was permanent—that the brain couldn't make new nerve cells to replace the dead ones. But a recent study reveals that after working out for three months, all the subjects appeared to sprout new neurons; those who gained the most in cardiovascular fitness also grew the most nerve cells. This, too, might be BDNF at work, transforming stem cells into full-grown, functional neurons.

6   Unlike neurogenesis, which can take weeks to occur, most of the additional effects of aerobic exercise appear almost immediately. Get off the treadmill after a half-hour workout, says Hillman, and "within 48 minutes" your brain will be in better shape. But alas, these benefits are somewhat transient. Like weight, mental fitness has to be maintained. New neurons, and the connections between them, will stick around for years, but within a month of inactivity, "the astrocytes shrink down again, and then the neurons don't function as well anymore," says William Greenough, a psychologist at the University of Illinois. Let your body go, then, and your brain will follow.

7   To keep the effects, you've got to keep working out. "If you're thinking that by exercising at age 20 you're going to have some effect on what you're like at age 70," Greenough adds, you'd better be willing to commit to 50 years of hitting the gym.

8   Finally, there's the question that's been dogging Charles Hillman since he first picked up a hockey stick: why, if jocks on average have more capable brains than the rest of the public, do they have an unfair reputation for being dumb? Why does a term like "scholar-athlete," which would have made so much sense to the ancient Greeks, get snickered at today? The reason, says Hillman, is found not in science but in common sense: some of our schools have failed young athletes by cutting them too much slack. "A lot of it comes from schools' giving them an easy road," he says. "Kids get this wholly inaccurate label because they're good at sports, and then too much emphasis is placed on their physical abilities at the expense of their mental abilities." Having a big, gorgeous, healthy brain isn't enough, of course; it also has to be full. For that, kids have to hit the library as well as the gym. "You can opti-

mize your brain to learn," says Ratey, "but then you have to be in an environment where you can do that—and you have to want it." Sometimes, it's the "scholar," not the "athlete," who counts.

Text B

Redheads Fear the Dentist, And Tall Men Get Cancer: What Your Appearance Says About Your Health

http://blog.newsweek.com/blogs/thehumancondition/archive/2009/08/26/redheads-fear-the-dentist-and-tall-men-get-cancer-what-your-appearance-says-about-your-health.aspx

By Cristina Goyanes Aug.26, 2009

1   Mirrors can tell us lots of things: whether that hangover from last night is showing in our faces, whether we've finally tamed that cowlick, whether our butts really do look big in those pants. But they can also give us a telling glimpse into what's going on below the surface.

2   Science suggests some physical traits may indicate clues about our health. Last week, for instance, American and German researchers published a study showing that tall men (6'3" and over) were 40 percent more likely to get an aggressive form of prostate cancer than men of average (5'7") height. This finding illustrated what researchers had long suspected: a report published in Cancer Epidemiology, Biomarkers & Prevention last year found that men's cancer risk increased by 6 percent for every additional 3.9-inch increase in height over the average, and that having longer legs increased the odds from 12 to 23 percent.

3   This finding had us thinking—what other seemingly innocent traits were connected to larger health issues? We collected five examples of how your body can spill secrets about your future health:

Being Tall: Cancer

4   Men aren't the only ones at risk: a study from Dutch researchers showed that women who were 5-feet, 9 inches or taller were also more likely to develop breast

cancer. Why this happens is still not understood, but it may have something to do with the production of a hormone, Insulin-Like Growth Factor-1. Rest assured: size doesn't matter too much. Or at least not enough to lose sleep over this slightly elevated risk.

Redheads: More Dental Pain

5   A study published in the Journal of the American Dental Association made news last month, showing that natural redheads carry a gene mutation that may affect their brain's ability to process pain-blocking meds like Novocain. Scientists still don't know what's happening in the bodies of people who have this melanocortin-1 receptor gene variation, but lead study author Catherine Binkley, DDS hopes that taking a blood sample or swabbing a cheek will let doctors know which patients are prone to anxiety—carriers were twice as likely to skip dental visits—and may require stronger anesthesia.

Dark skinned individuals: May develop nasty smoking habit, eventual cancer

6   People who have a dark complexion—thanks to genetics or tanning—are more likely to develop nicotine dependence, which, ultimately, may lead to tobacco-specific diseases, says a study published in *Pharmacology, Biochemistry and Behavior*. Previous lab work had already established that nicotine binds to melanin, a tissue that determines the pigmentation of one's skin. Building on that, Pennsylvania State University researchers discovered that when nicotine bonds to high concentrations of melanin, it metabolizes at a slower rate throughout the day opposed to the average two hours.

7   "Dark-skinned people smoke fewer cigarettes than their lighter-skinned counterparts because they are satiated longer," says lead investigator Gary King. "However, we believe that some carcinogens are also binding and remaining in the body longer as well. This may help explain why African Americans have a higher incidence of smoking-related cancers," he adds.

Men with asymmetrical faces: More likely to have dementia

8   Not even the best poker face can hide the fact that men with crooked grins may

experience a blackout in brainpower one day. An article published in the journal *Evolution and Human Behavior* discovered that the men who had asymmetrical faces—the left side didn't mirror the right—were more likely to develop dementia than those with well-balanced mugs.

9 Using 216 photographs of men and women between the ages of 79 and 83, researchers measured 15 facial landmarks, including the corners of the eyes and mouth as well as the side of the nose and chin points. "Facial symmetry, just like body symmetry, is thought to be an indicator of developmental stability," says Lars Penke, the study author. "If one side grows smaller or larger than the other, this means that something has gone a little wrong, that the development was disrupted, for example by exposure to pathogens, toxins or radiation, by malnutrition or by genetic mutations."

10 Only men, not women, showed the connection between a lack of symmetry and senility. Why the gender discrepancy? Perhaps it's because women generally live longer and take better care of their bodies, says Penke who encourages everyone— male or female, droopy face or no—to cultivate a healthy body in order to keep a sharp mind.

Long ring fingers: Great in bed, at risk for osteoarthritis

11 How's this for palm reading: If your ring finger is longer than your index finger you may be twice as likely to develop osteoarthritis, say British researchers. In the past, the index and ring finger ratio has been linked to good things: higher sperm count, athletic ability, and sexual prowess. But this article published in the journal *Arthritis & Rheumatism* is the first to find a connection between the digit ratio and hip and knee problems.

12 Researchers took radiographs of the knees, hips, and hands of more than 3,000 people, most of whom had a history of below the waist joint issues. What they discovered was that those whose index finger was shorter than their ring were at greater risk of knee osteoarthritis. This was especially true for women, who generally have equal sized second and fourth fingers. Why? Again, still a mystery. These studies are designed to find signifiers or common traits in those who have a disease, but aren't always able to speculate why those traits influence health.

Section C After Reading

I. Vocabulary Builder

1. Do NOT consult the dictionary, and guess the meanings of the underlined words by the context, word formation, grammar, general knowledge, or any other skills you can rely on.

   The following items are for Text A:

   1) The film is full of **_stereotypes_**: a stupid blonde, a fat American tourist, and a gay man with huge muscles.

   2) She told him Jeff was just a friend, and he was **_dumb_** enough to believe her.

   3) That **_jock_** thinks he's the king of the world because he's popular, but he's gonna end up being a loser flipping burgers at McDonalds.

   4) His daily **_routine_** consisted of work, dinner, then TV and bed, which he follows for 20 years.

   5) If you think there's something wrong about the situation, you should trust your **_intuition_**.

   6) Like the Eight Immortals crossing the sea, each one shows his or her special **_prowess_**.

   7) The human resource department gives each applicant the opportunity to **_demonstrate_** whether they are suited to the work.

   8) Further research has resulted in a more **_profound_** appreciation of the problem.

   9) We waited at the **_junction_** of Fulton Street and Gough Avenue for the lights to change.

2. Read through **Text B** and find the English counterparts of the following Chinese words or phrases.

   1) 前列腺癌   2) 看似无害的体征
   3) 乳腺癌   4) 荷尔蒙
   5) 基因突变   6) 采血样
   7) 更强力的麻醉剂   8) 尼古丁成瘾

9）尼古丁与黑色素结合 10）以更缓慢的速度代谢
11）美国黑人 12）面无表情
13）营养不良 14）性别差异
15）看手相 16）无名指
17）食指 18）更高的精子数
19）学术期刊 20）手指比率

3. Complete the sentences using words given in the box, change forms when necessary.

| be prone to | boost | counterpart | derive | illustrate |
| nourish | permanent | snicker | speculate | transient |

1) Bars in Madrid offer more and better food than their American _____.
2) The cream contains vitamin A to _____ the skin.
3) About a quarter of the drugs in prescription medicines today are _____ from plants.
4) Most police departments keep a (n) _____ record of all violent crimes committed in their area.
5) He knew they _____ behind his back, but he believed that they would eventually accept him as one of their own.
6) Greater consumer access to the Internet has _____ electronic retailing.
7) Edward began to _____ on what life would be like if he were single again.
8) Let me give an example to _____ the point.
9) He _____ lose his temper when people disagree with him.
10) Once the _____ sleep problem has passed, stop taking the sleeping pills.

II. Sentence Translation

1. Every time a bicep or quad contracts and releases, it sends out chemicals, including a protein called IGF-1 that travels through the bloodstream, across the blood-brain barrier and into the brain itself. (Para. 3, Text A)

_____

_____

2. This is the process that underlies learning: every change in the junctions between brain cells signifies a new fact or skill that's been picked up and stowed away for future use. (Para. 4, Text A)

3. "If you're thinking that by exercising at age 20 you're going to have some effect on what you're like at age 70," Greenough adds, you'd better be willing to commit to 50 years of hitting the gym. (Para. 7, Text A)

4. Mirrors can tell us lots of things: whether that hangover from last night is showing in our faces, whether we've finally tamed that cowlick, whether our butts really do look big in those pants. But they can also give us a telling glimpse into what's going on below the surface. (Para. 1, Text B)

III. Comprehension of the Texts

Answer the following questions.

Questions 1—8 are for Text A:

1. What is Charles Hillman?
2. What is Charles Hillman's new academic finding?
3. According to the traditional theory, why is there a body-brain interaction?
4. What is BDNF? And what can increase the production of it?
5. How does BDNF do its job of increasing learning ability?
6. What is the other function of BDNF except for increasing learning ability?
7. How to understand "Let your body go, then your brain will follow" (Para. 7)?
8. What makes the sportsmen always considered stupid if they should be smarter than common people?

Questions 9—15 are for Text B:

9. Which example of body-health relationship is limited just to man?
10. What is the possible cause of cancer caused by being tall?
11. How can a dentist know whether a patient is pain tolerant or pain sensitive?
12. Why can nicotine stay longer in dark-skinned people's body than the lighter-skinned people's?
13. Guess the meaning of "asymmetrical" and "dementia" in the fourth subtitle.
14. Guess the meaning of the word "osteoarthritis" in the fifth subtitle.
15. Why did most of the studies fail to discover a definite reason to explain these appearance-health connections?

Unit 12
Automobile & Driving

Section A Before Reading

Part One Lead-in

A headline is the text at the top of a newspaper article, indicating the nature of the article below it. Headlines are written in much larger type size than the article text, and often in a different font entirely. Headline conventions include normally using present tense even when discussing events that happened in the recent past; omitting forms of the verb "to be" in certain contexts; and removing short articles like "a" and "the". Most newspapers feature a very large headline on their front page, dramatically describing the biggest news of the day. Words chosen for headlines are often short, giving rise to headlines. A headline may also be followed by a smaller secondary headline, often called subhead or "deck hed", which gives more information.

The film *The Shipping News* has an illustrative exchange between the protagonist, who is learning how to write for a local newspaper, and his publisher:

Publisher: It's finding the center of your story, the beating heart of it, that's what makes a reporter. You have to start by making up some headlines. You know: short, punchy, dramatic headlines. Now, have a look, [*pointing at dark clouds gathering in the sky over the ocean*]. What do you see? Tell me the headline:

Protagonist: HORIZON FILLS WITH DARK CLOUDS?

Publisher: IMMINENT STORM THREATENS VILLAGE.

Protagonist: BUT WHAT IF NO STORM COMES?

Publisher: VILLAGE SPARED FROM DEADLY STORM.

Part Two Warm-up Questions

1. Should people all round the world drive on the same side of the road?

2. Do you think it's necessary for you to learn how to drive in China? Why or not?

3. Which would you like to possess, a domestic or a foreign brand car?

Section B Texts Reading

Text A

Why Don't We All Drive on the Same Side of the Road?

http://www.time.com/time/world/article/0,8599,1920427,00.html

By Randy James   Sept.5, 2009

1   Residents of Samoa are bracing for chaos this month as the Pacific island nation becomes the first country in decades to order motorists to start driving on the opposite side of the road. On the morning of Sept. 7, drivers will switch from the right side of the street—where about two-thirds of the world's traffic moves—to the left, in order to open the nation to low-cost used autos from left-driving Australia and New Zealand. It will mark the world's first road switch since Ghana, Nigeria and Sierra Leone changed sides in the 1970s, and one of the only instances of switching from the right to the left; virtually every other change has been the reverse. Worried about increased accidents, tens of thousands of Samoans have protested the plan. As a Samoan lawyer opposed to the switch told the *Times* of London, "Cars are going to crash,

people are going to die, not to mention the huge expense to our small country."

2　　　It remains a curiosity and a bit of a historical mystery why the world is divided over something as basic as which side of the road to drive on. The fact that most people are right-handed has a lot to do with it; that's why, for much of history, travelers have stuck to the left. Ancient Romans using chariots are believed to have held the reins with their right hands and a whip with their left; to avoid whipping oncoming drivers, they favored the left-hand side of the road (called "left-hand traffic"). It's also easier for right-handers to mount a horse from the left, so riders gravitated to that side to avoid oncoming traffic as they climbed on and off. Finally, knights and other armed travelers favored the left so they could do battle, if necessary, with their good hand.

3　　　So why does most of the world travel on the right side today? Theories differ, but there's no doubt Napoleon was a major influence. The French have used the right since at least the late 18th century (there's evidence of a Parisian "keep-right" law dating to 1794). Some say that before the French Revolution, aristocrats drove their carriages on the left, forcing the peasantry to the right. Amid the upheaval, fearful aristocrats sought to blend in with the proletariat by traveling on the right as well. Regardless of the origin, Napoleon brought right-hand traffic to the nations he conquered, including Russia, Switzerland and Germany. Hitler, in turn, ordered right-hand traffic in Czechoslovakia and Austria in the 1930s. Nations that escaped right-handed conquest, like Great Britain, preserved their left-handed tradition.

4　　　The U.S. has not always been a nation of right-hand drivers; earlier in its history, carriage and horse traffic traveled on the left, as it did in England. But by the late 1700s, the theory goes, teamsters driving large wagons pulled by several pairs of horses began prompting a shift to the right. A driver would sit on the rear left horse in order to wield his whip with his right hand; to see opposite traffic clearly, the teamsters traveled on the right.

5　　　One of the final moves to firmly standardize traffic directions in the U.S. occurred in the 20th century, when Henry Ford decided to mass-produce his cars with controls on the left (one reason, stated in a 1908 catalog: the convenience for passengers exiting directly onto the curb, "especially ... if there is a lady to be considered"). Once these norms were set, many countries eventually adjusted to conform to the right-hand standard, including Canada in the 1920s, Sweden in 1967 and Burma in 1970. The U. K. and former colonies such as Australia and India are among the Western world's few remaining holdouts. Several Asian nations, including Japan, use the left as well—a possible legacy of samurai warriors who wore their swords on their left and didn't want to bump anyone—though many places use both right-hand-drive and left-hand-drive cars.

6   Despite widespread opposition to the changeover in Samoa, the government insists it's prepared for the move. Officials have added road humps to slow traffic and, according to the *Wall Street Journal*, set up a training area near a sports stadium where people can practice driving on the flip side. Sept. 7 and 8 have been declared national holidays to help people ease into the new law. Leau Apisaloma, a village chief, told the *Journal* there's no cause for alarm: "In the beginning, it will be hard, but we'll learn—we're not stupid."

Text B

A special report on China and America

Tug-of-car

Detroit's and China's carmakers both want a piece of the action

http://www.economist.com/specialreports/displaystory.cfm?story_id=14678523
From *The Economist* Oct. 22, 2009

1   "Shanghai, Guangzhou, Changchun, Beijing, Wuhan, Chongqing: six cities with six dreams. But what they really all dream of is the same—Detroit." So concluded an article on the rival centres of China's fast-growing car industry published by one of China's leading newspapers, *21st Century Business Herald*. That was a long five years ago. Now Detroit dreams of China.

2   Earlier this year, as the American government was buying 61% of General Motors and 8% of Chrysler to prevent them from collapsing, the two manufacturers' sales in China were rocketing. Indeed, China's car market was overtaking America's

in sales volume for the first time (see the chart below), several years earlier than analysts had predicted before the financial crisis. Plummeting demand in the West was to blame.

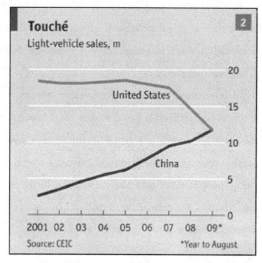

3   GM's sales in China in August more than doubled on a year earlier. For 2009 as a whole the company predicted a 40% rise. Sales of all car brands in China in August were about 90% up, helped by a cut in the purchase tax on smaller, more fuel-efficient cars. There is huge pent-up demand as a new middle class takes to the road.

4   The Chinese government wants to emulate America's rise to industrial glory by making the car industry a pillar of economic growth. This is a boon to foreign carmakers—not least American ones—which have formed joint ventures with Chinese state-owned companies to build their cars in China. The relentless growth of cities and huge government spending on expressways offer prospects for carmakers reminiscent of those in America in the mid-20th century.

5   The sales figures may be impressive, but the benefits to American car companies' bottom lines are far less so. One senior manager of a Detroit carmaker says that rather than actual profits, China offers more in the way of psychological solace for companies eager to show they can still do business. The boom in China is generating far less revenue for American car manufacturers than the growth in car sales in Europe did in the 1990s, he notes. The cars selling fastest in China—as the government intended—are the smaller models with the lowest profit margins.

6   But China still offers huge potential, not only because its citizens will get richer and upgrade their cars, but also eventually—or so China likes to believe—as a base for producing cars at low cost and selling them into developed markets. "The irony is that some of the first cars that the Chinese export might have an American brand name on them," says Stephen Biegun, a senior manager at Ford.

7   Another possibility is that some American brand names will become Chinese. Dollar-rich China, encouraged by the financial crisis, is telling its companies to look abroad for bargains. A little-known private company from Sichuan Province, Sichuan Tengzhong Heavy Industrial Machinery, earlier this month reached a deal with GM to buy its Hummer brand (subject to Chinese government approval). A state-owned company, Beijing Automotive Industry Holding, is planning to join a Swedish-led consortium in a bid for GM's Saab unit. Geely, a private company, is looking at Ford's Volvo operation. Buying a foreign brand makes sense for Chinese car firms, which have little international reputation or experience of their own. Quality and safety issues have proved enormous barriers for Chinese brands trying to enter Western markets.

8   Just as Japanese carmakers rattled the American car industry in the 1970s, the arrival of Chinese makers, though not yet imminent, will be upsetting for some when it comes. The United Auto Workers union (UAW), which represents the Big Three's blue-collar car workers, was outraged when GM said earlier this year that it was planning to make the Chevrolet Spark, a subcompact car, in China and ship it to America. Many politicians sided with the union, pointing out that the company was

majority-owned by the American government. "If you're going to build them in China, sell them in China," says the UAW's president, Ron Gettelfinger.

Buy American

9   Chinese companies buying American ones will also cause anxiety. In 2005 the plan of a Chinese state-owned company, CNOOC, to buy an American oil company, Unocal, sparked widespread fury among American politicians. They worried, mistakenly, that America would lose a strategic asset. CNOOC meekly withdrew its $18 billion bid. "It's not necessarily the Chinese [government] making decisions," says Ford's Mr Biegun. "It is the Chinese people and Chinese companies." Politicians, however, have so far been muted in their response to the possible sale of Hummer, a gas-guzzling, loss-making brand. These days, what counts is keeping jobs.

10   Jim Farley, who is in charge of marketing at Ford, says that "over time the whole industry absolutely has to be prepared" for the day when finished cars will be shipped from China to America. The industry should "welcome that with open arms", he insists. Another car executive says it may not make sense to set up dedicated factories in China to serve the American market, but production lines in China could be used to plug gaps in supply that might open up in America.

11   American consumers might be slow to embrace Chinese-branded vehicles, which so far have made inroads only in emerging markets that care more about price than quality. But the Chinese government sees an opportunity in hybrid and other "green" cars, demand for which is likely to grow fast. With its economies of scale and abundant labour, China is hoping to gain an edge in what promises to be a lucrative new industry.

12   That would help to brighten the environmentally gloomy prospect of a China moving towards American levels of car ownership. Sceptics say China is unlikely to mandate the use of new fuel technologies so early in the development of its car industry. Others disagree. China, says one American car executive, could leapfrog ahead in adopting cleaner car fuels, especially batteries, for which it already has a strong manufacturing base. "I do think they are going to be formidable competitors," she says. The UAW may one day have to brace itself.

Section C After Reading

I. *Vocabulary Builder*

1. Do NOT consult the dictionary, and guess the meanings of the underlined words by the context, word formation, grammar, general knowledge, or any other skills you can rely on.

   The following items are for Text A:

   1) You had better *brace* yourself—I have some bad news.

   2) Meanwhile, Sean tied the *reins* of his horse to the fence before running towards his house.

   3) The pause in the taxi became so long that the female taxi driver looked anxiously at her passenger, his face illuminated by the headlights of *oncoming* cars.

   4) The lights suddenly turned off and it took a few seconds for her eyes to *adjust* to the darkness.

   5) When the poles *flip*—a process that takes several hundred thousand years—the magnetic field rapidly regains its strength and the cycle is repeated.

2. Read through **Text B** and find the English counterparts of the following Chinese words or phrases.

   1) 低油耗的车   2) 合资企业
   3) 国企   4) 底线
   5) 心理安慰   6) 最低的利润空间
   7) 私企   8) 经中国政府同意
   9) 低端紧凑型轿车   10) 战略资产
   11) 填补空白   12) 新兴市场
   13) 氢动力车   14) 获得优势
   15) 获利丰厚的新兴工业   16) 强大的对手

3. Complete the sentences using words given in the box, change forms when necessary.

bid	brace	emulate	gravitate	imminent	mandate
mute	overtake	preserve	plummet	prompt	mount
relentless	reverse	spark	switch	upheaval	

1) The incident so shocked all the students that it _____ further protest.

2) Developing countries often try to _____ experiences of developed countries, but this is not always a good idea.

3) Parents should avoid hanging a dark cloud by communicating that life is dangerous and that failure is _____.

4) The question was like a blow, causing Roz to _____ herself against the sofa.

5) Retail sales of the quintessential red meats are _____, whilst vegetarianism has become a fashionable norm.

6) He _____ easily and fluently from speaking English to French to German.

7) Lewis is known as a difficult interview subject, but my own experience with him was quite the _____.

8) Television soon _____ the cinema as the most popular form of entertainment.

9) Nuclear power has always been a topic that has _____ off considerable debate.

10) A number of companies have submitted _____ to buy the supermarket chain.

11) As the dispute continues, tension is _____ on the border between the two countries.

12) There was always plenty to drink, and eventually the two would _____ toward each other and dance very close.

13) Ridge's success is due to a(n) _____ pursuit of perfection.

14) Now, however, a series of social _____ since 1970 have caused changes in the consciousness of the people.

15) All the names in the book have been changed to _____ the victims' anonymity.

16) What exactly _____ him to call you in the middle of the night?

17) The state _____ that high school students take three years of English.

II. Sentence Translation

1. Some say that before the French Revolution, aristocrats drove their carriages on the left, forcing the peasantry to the right. Amid the upheaval, fearful aristocrats sought to blend in with the proletariat by traveling on the right as well. (Para. 3, Text A)

2. Several Asian nations, including Japan, use the left as well—a possible legacy of samurai warriors who wore their swords on their left and didn't want to bump anyone—though many places use both right-hand-drive and left-hand-drive cars. (Para. 5, Text A)

3. The Chinese government wants to emulate America's rise to industrial glory by making the car industry a pillar of economic growth. (Para. 4, Text B)

4. The relentless growth of cities and huge government spending on expressways offer prospects for carmakers reminiscent of those in America in the mid-20th century. (Para. 4, Text B)

5. Another car executive says it may not make sense to set up dedicated factories in China to serve the American market, but production lines in China could be used to plug gaps in supply that might open up in America. (Para. 10, Text B)

III. Comprehension of the Texts

Answer the following questions.

Questions 1—10 are for Text A:

1. What happened in Samoa?
2. Why does Samoa government make that change?
3. What makes the new change in Samoa so unique?
4. How does people response to the new traffic law in Samoa?
5. What are the reasons for ancient people to ride on the left side of the road?
6. What is the common measure both Napoleon and Hitler took to make the right-side travel dominate the world?
7. Why did the American teamsters shift to the right side of the road according to the theory?
8. What is the dominant ingredient of the standardization of right-hand-drive?
9. Which countries still drive on the left hand side of the road according to the news report?
10. What preparations does the government make to adopt people to the new traffic law?

Questions 11—16 are for Text B:

11. Why did the car sales in China increase in August?
12. Why does the high sales volume in China not lead to high profits for American carmakers?
13. Why does the China's industry market hold a huge potential?
14. Why is it necessary for Chinese car firmer to buy western car brands?
15. Who will be upset due to the approach of Chinese carmakers and why?
16. What are the attitudes of Americans towards China's prospect of environmental friendly cars?

Unit 13

Quality Problems

Section A Before Reading

Part One Lead-in

The New York Times is an American daily newspaper founded in 1851 and published in New York City. The largest metropolitan newspaper in the United States, "The Gray Lady"—named for its staid appearance and style—is regarded as a national newspaper of record. The *Times* is owned by The New York Times Company, which publishes eighteen other newspapers, including the *International Herald Tribune* and *The Boston Globe*.

The paper's motto, as printed in the upper left-hand corner of the front page, is "All the News That's Fit to Print." It is organized into sections: News, Opinions, Business, Arts, Science, Sports, Style, and Features. When referring to people, the *Times* generally uses honorifics, rather than unadorned last names (except in the sports pages, book review and magazine). The newspaper's headlines tend to be verbose, and, for major stories, come with subheadings giving further details, although it is moving away from this style. It stayed with an eight-column format until September 1976, years after other papers had switched to six, and it was one of the last newspapers to adopt color photography, with the first color photograph on the front page appearing on October 16, 1997. In the absence of a major headline, the day's most important story generally appears in the top-right hand column, on the main page.

The *Times* has won 101 Pulitzer Prizes, the most of any news organization. Its website was the most popular American online newspaper Website as of December 2008, receiving more than 18 million unique visitors in that month. The *Times* prices are: $2.00 daily city and nationwide, $5.00 Sunday in and around the city, $6.00 or $7.00 outside of the metropolitan area.

Part Two Warm-up Questions

1. Have you experienced any quality problem in your life? Give one example.
2. How do you deal with the quality problem when you are confronted with one?
3. What do you think of China's quality protection system?

Section B Texts Reading

Text A

Death Sentences in China Milk Case

http://www.nytimes.com/2009/01/22/news/22iht-23MILK.19584434.html
By Mark McDonald Jan. 22, 2009

1 Hong Kong—Two men were sentenced to death on Thursday and the chairwoman of a dairy conglomerate received a life sentence for their roles in the contaminated-milk scandal that killed six children and sickened nearly 300,000, according to Xinhua, the official Chinese news agency.

2 Tian Wenhua, the former head of Sanlu, the milk company at the center of the scandal, was sentenced to life in prison. All the deaths in the milk scandal so far have been linked to her company.

3 The initial verdicts Thursday were among the first in the high-profile trial of 21 defendants implicated in the scandal over milk products and infant formula contaminated with melamine. The industrial chemical, normally used in the production of fertilizer and plastics, was added to milk to falsely raise protein levels in tests.

4 Melamine can cause kidney stones and other ailments, especially in young children. More than 800 children remain hospitalized in China due to melamine-related illnesses, according to the Ministry of Health.

5 The trial is being held before the Intermediate People's Court in Shijiazhuang, in the northern province of Hebei, where Sanlu is based. The company, whose busi-

ness crumbled after the scandal first broke in September, is now in bankruptcy proceedings.

6   Ms. Tian pleaded guilty on Dec. 31, the opening day of the case. Her plea acknowledged for the first time that Sanlu knew of the problem months long before it alerted local officials.

7   Chinese state-controlled media broadcast images of Tian, 66, looking pale and contrite, standing handcuffed before a microphone in a yellow smock acknowledging her guilt.

8   Xinhua reported that Zhang Yujun received one of the death penalties for producing and selling melamine-laced "protein powder." Prosecutors said Mr. Zhang, a cattleman from Hebei Province, concocted the powder by mixing melamine and malt starch. He allegedly made nearly 800 tons of the powder, from October 2007 through August of last year.

9   The other man sentenced to death, Geng Jinping, was convicted of producing and selling toxic food, Xinhua said.

10   Wang Yuliang, another former Sanlu executive on trial, has appeared in court with a wheelchair. State-run media outlets said he tried to commit suicide in 2008.

11   In 2007, after earlier product-safety scandals, the head of China's State Food and Drug Administration was executed after he was found guilty of corruption and dereliction of duty as a regulator.

12   Last Saturday, the parents of a 6-month-old boy who died in May from drinking tainted formula accepted a cash payment from Sanlu.

13   The parents, Yi Yongsheng and Jiao Hongfang, were the first to receive compensation for the death of a child in the milk scandal. They accepted more than $29,200 from Sanlu, according to their lawyer, Dong Junming.

14   As part of the compensation deal, the parents have agreed to drop a lawsuit they filed in October against Sanlu in Gansu Province, where the family lives. The court, the Lanzhou Intermediate People's Court, did not accept the case.

15   Also, a group of lawyers said Tuesday they had filed a lawsuit against a group of dairy companies on behalf of the families of 213 children who died or fell ill from drinking tainted milk. The filing is a rare instance in which Chinese lawyers are proceeding with a class-action product liability case.

16   The lawsuit, seeking more than $5.2 million in compensation, was filed last week with the Supreme People's Court in Beijing, said Lin Zheng, an administrator for a group of lawyers who have volunteered to represent the victims' families.

17   The compensation amounts being demanded vary case by case, with the largest being $73,000 for a dead child, Lin said in an interview with *The New York Times*.

18   It was unclear whether the court intended to accept the lawsuit.

19   The 213 victims in the latest lawsuit include four dead children who have not been included in the government's official death toll, Lin said. The lawyers are also preparing a lawsuit concerning a fifth unacknowledged dead child, he added.

20   A woman answering the phone at the office of the China Dairy Industry Association said the association had no comment on the lawsuit.

David Barboza contributed reporting from Shanghai and Edward Wong from Beijing.

Text B

Is Drywall the Next Chinese Import Scandal?

http://www.time.com/time/nation/article/0,8599,1887059,00.html
By Tim Padgett Mar. 23, 2009

Howard Ehrsam of Chinese Drywall Screening removes an electrical plate to see if the receptacles show any signs of Chinese drywall in a home in Port St. Lucie, Fla.

1   Soon after Danie Beck and her husband bought their two-story town house west of Miami in the summer of 2006, she thought an animal had died somewhere behind the walls. The strong sulfurous odor lingered, she says, and she began having dizzy spells that would keep her in bed for days. She began suffering from insomnia and sore, swollen joints. The house, too, appeared to be ailing: lights began blinking on and off, and Beck noticed discoloration of her wood furniture. The air conditioner, an indispensable appliance in South Florida, kept conking out. "It was an absolute nightmare," the 67-year-old dance teacher says. "I felt as if something in this house was hammering me into the ground every day."

2   It wasn't until her repairman got fed up with fixing inexplicably corroded air-conditioner coils that Beck finally discovered what she and her home builder suspect is the source of the poltergeist: the Chinese drywall inside the house. Beck is among hundreds of homeowners in Florida alleging that toxic levels of chemical pollutants like sulfur are issuing from contaminated drywall made in some Chinese factories. At

least four class actions have been filed in Florida; others have been filed in California, Louisiana and Alabama.

3   The U.S. Consumer Product Safety Commission is investigating the complaints. If the drywall proves to be the culprit, plaintiffs' attorneys say tens of thousands of potentially affected homes could see a further drop in prices already hammered by the credit crisis. "A lot of these people are just getting hit over the head a second time," says David Durkee, a Miami attorney who has filed one of the suits. "This could have a further impact on the mortgage crisis by giving overwhelmed homeowners another incentive to just walk away from their houses."

4   During the heady but reckless days of the recent U.S. housing-construction boom, builders were desperate for materials, and drywall was especially in demand. Before 2005, drywall imports to the U.S. from China were negligible; since 2006, more than 550 million lb. of it has been shipped here, mostly to Florida. The imports amount to a fraction of the 15 million tons of drywall produced domestically each year, but it was used to build more than 60,000 homes in at least a dozen states—including some post-Katrina reconstruction in Louisiana.

5   More than half the homes built with Chinese drywall are in Florida. Some of the suits there target construction companies; others include German drywall manufacturer Knauf and its Chinese subsidiaries—which are in turn being sued by at least one Florida home builder, Lennar Corp. Miami-based Lennar, which is also suing the U.S. suppliers from which it bought the Chinese drywall, has confronted the problem and initiated a program to do inspections and remove the offending wallboard in many homes, including Beck's. (The process usually involves moving a family out of the house for at least six months to replace its interior.) Another lawsuit defendant, Engle Homes, based in Hollywood, Fla., has also admitted that the drywall problem exists in at least a small number of its homes. In a statement about houses near Fort Myers, Fla., that are part of Durkee's suit, the company says, "Our initial findings tell us that this seems to be an isolated incident that has affected a small number of Engle Homes in the Fort Myers, Fla., area and we are currently developing a plan to assist our affected homeowners."

6   Drywall is made from gypsum, a soft mineral, that is pressed between thick pa-

perboard. Plaintiffs' attorneys say the allegedly toxic drywall material probably originated in at least one gypsum mine in China and possibly others. (A few years ago, Knauf and other drywall producers received complaints about a mine in Tianjin, China; Knauf says it stopped using the mine toward the end of 2006.) But Knauf denies that its product is toxic and argues it is not the only supplier of Chinese-made drywall to the U.S. Contacted by *TIME*, the company referred to a statement by its subsidiary, Knauf Plasterboard Tianjin Ltd.: "Any low levels of sulfur compounds present in the air in homes are not a health risk ... The substances identified in testing are in no greater amounts than [in] the air found outside homes or in soil, marshes or the oceans."

7 The Florida Department of Health has not yet concluded its own tests of the drywall in question. But Beck and other homeowners insist the common symptoms suffered by the Chinese-drywalled houses and their occupants can't be mere coincidence. The problem came to light last year as those homeowners began commiserating on the Internet about rotten-egg smells in their houses and rashes of nosebleeds and other ailments. At the same time, exasperated air-conditioner repairmen began complaining to builders about copper-coil corrosion in newly built houses. The air-conditioning companies concluded it was caused by high levels of airborne sulfur and moldy toxins. Wires in <u>outlets</u>, appliances and lamps were going bad too, as was wood. That in turn raised red flags for consumer-protection groups, already alarmed in recent years by the flood of defective Chinese-made products like toothpaste and toys.

8 Depending on how many homes ultimately prove to be contaminated, the repair costs—Beck says Lennar promised to tear her house down "to the studs"—could run into the tens of millions for builders. And that does not include the unspecified damages sought in the lawsuits. One problem plaintiffs face, however, is that many of the builders being sued have gone bankrupt in the recent housing bust. And even if homes are repaired, they may still carry the <u>taint</u> of having been drywall victims. Beck paid $344,000 for her town house; it is now worth $245,000—less than the amount owed on her mortgage. And she worries that she may not be able to sell it at some point in the future even after Lennar fixes the drywall problem. "I'll admit

there are moments when I'm tempted to ask Lennar to just buy the house back," says Beck, whose husband died last year of cancer. (His illness was not related to the drywall.)

9   Beck's fortunes have taken a pummeling in recent years. She and her husband bought the town house after an arson fire destroyed the Miami home they had lived in for 39 years. And she has become accustomed to seeing its value jeopardized by the threat of hurricanes and by Wall Street malfeasance. But she wasn't expecting any trouble from China.

Section C   After Reading

I. Vocabulary Builder

1. Read through Text A and B and find the English counterparts of the following Chinese words or phrases.

   The following items are for Text A:

   1) 被判死刑   2) 终身监禁
   3) 毒奶粉丑闻   4) 高调的审判
   5) 被告   6) 婴儿配方
   7) 提高蛋白质含量   8) 肾结石
   9) 认罪   10) 公诉人
   11) 玩忽职守   12) 赔偿协议
   13) 撤诉   14) 上诉
   15) 对产品质量问题的集体诉讼案   16) 官方死亡人数

   The following items are for Text B:

   17) 移开墙壁电板   18) 浓烈的硫磺味挥之不去
   19) 木质家具褪色   20) 必不可少的家电
   21) 令人费解的空调线圈腐蚀   22) 原告律师
   23) 信贷危机   24) 建筑公司
   25) 石膏矿   26) 问题暴露
   27) 引起警觉   28) 未详细说明的损失

2. Complete the sentences using words given in the box, change forms when necessary.

ailment	confront	contaminate	corroded
execute	implicate	initiated	negligible
overwhelm	reckless	subsidiary	tempted

1) Five others who had been _____, including the head of National Security, were not prosecuted, allegedly due to political considerations.
2) The food was _____ by an infected worker during the production process.
3) The medicine was supposed to cure all kinds of _____, ranging from colds to back pains.
4) This is a backward and cruel society, in which people are _____ for homosexuality and adultery.
5) Over the years, rain, wind, and sun had _____ the statue, turning the bronze a bright green.
6) Sometimes a sense of deep frustration almost _____ her.
7) If there was no insurance, would they be more likely to take better care of themselves, and would the cost of medical treatment, car repairs, etc. go down? Does insurance encourage _____ behavior?
8) Also, strikes are responsible for an almost _____ amount of lost time compared with total hours worked by the employed population.
9) Under our law, a(n) _____ can go bankrupt and normally the parent company will not be liable for its debts.
10) Their lives were now _____ by earthshaking change, by the arrival of the modern world.
11) Dr. Endsleigh _____ a number of projects for disabled children, but has now moved on to work in the Third World.
12) The gallery looks so much like a cocktail lounge you may be _____ to ask a guard for a martini.

3. Study the following synonyms and fill in each of the blanks with one from the box, change forms when necessary.

If you want to say 动机, you can use:

> a) **incentive**: [cn., un.] *something that encourages you to work harder, start new activities, etc.*
>
> b) **motive**: [cn.] *the reason that makes someone decide to do something, esp. something bad or dishonest*
>
> c) **motivation**: [un.] *the strong feeling that is your reason for wanting to do something or achieve something, esp. something that may take a long time to achieve*

1) She enjoyed the excitement of her work. Money was not her only _____.

2) The government is offering special tax _____ to people wanting to start up small businesses.

3) People are beginning to question the political _____ behind the decision to release the prisoners.

II. Sentence Translation

1. In 2007, after earlier product-safety scandals, the head of China's State Food and Drug Administration was executed after he was found guilty of corruption and dereliction of duty as a regulator. (Para. 11, Text A)

_____

_____

2. It wasn't until her repairman got fed up with fixing inexplicably corroded air-conditioner coils that Beck finally discovered what she and her home builder suspect is the source of the poltergeist: the Chinese drywall inside the house. (Para. 2, Text B)

_____

_____

3. "A lot of these people are just getting hit over the head a second time," says a Miami attorney. "This could have a further impact on the mortgage crisis by giv-

ing overwhelmed homeowners another incentive to just walk away from their houses." (Para. 3, Text B)

4. The imports amount to a fraction of the 15 million tons of drywall produced domestically each year, but it was used to build more than 60,000 homes in at least a dozen states—including in some post-Katrina reconstruction in Louisiana. (Para. 4, Text B)

5. Contacted by *TIME*, the company referred to a statement by its subsidiary Knauf Plasterboard Tianjin Ltd.: "Any low levels of sulfur compounds present in the air in homes are not a health risk ... The substances identified in testing are in no greater amounts than [in] the air found outside homes or in soil, marshes or the oceans." (Para. 6, Text B)

III. Comprehension of the Texts

Answer the following questions.

Questions 1—5 are for Text A:

1. What is this trial about?
2. How many defendants were mentioned by name in the news? And what did they commit in the Sanlu case?
3. Which court is the trial being held at?
4. Which case does the underlined words "the case" in Paragraph 14 refer to?
5. Which lawsuit has been filed to the Supreme People's Court in Beijing?

Questions 6—15 are for Text B:

6. What do we know from Paragraph 1?
7. Where are the problems with Beck and her house coming from?
8. What are the possible consequences if the drywall issue is proved to be true?

9. What is the reason for America to import more drywall from China since 2006?
10. Which defendants of the Florida drywall lawsuits are mentioned? And who are they?
11. What are the reactions of the different defendants in Florida drywall suits?
12. Summarize the main idea of Paragraph 7.
13. What are the worries of the owners of the drywall-polluted houses?
14. The underlined word "outlets" appears both in Paragraph 10, Text A and Paragraph 7, Text B. What does it mean respectively?
15. The underlined word "taint" appears both in Paragraph 12, Text A and Paragraph 8, Text B. Do they belong to the same word class? And why?

Unit 14

Shopping

Section A Before Reading

Part One Lead-in

Imelda Marcos is the widow of the 10th President of Philippines, Ferdinand Marcos, and is herself an influential political figure. She is notorious for her extravagant lifestyle, and her crazy love for shoes. She responded to criticisms of her extravagance by claiming that it was her "duty" to be "some kind of light, a star to give [the poor] guidelines." In February 1986, her husband was overthrown in the famous People Power Revolution and then they fled the Philippines. After the Marcos family fled Malacañang Palace, Marcos was found to have left behind 15 mink coats, 508 gowns, 1000 handbags and 3000 pairs of shoes.

Nero was the fifth and last Roman emperor of the Julio-Claudian dynasty. And he is sort of related to the Great Fire of Rome erupted in AD 64. The fire burned for over five days. It completely destroyed four of fourteen Roman districts and severely damaged seven. It is uncertain who or what actually caused the fire—whether accident or arson. Some historians favor Nero as the arsonist, so he could build a new palace. Popular legend claims that Nero even played the fiddle and sang songs at the time of the fire.

Augeas: In Greek mythology, Augeas was king of Elis. He is best known for his stables, which housed the single greatest number of cattle in the country and had never been cleaned—until the time of the great hero Heracles. The fifth of the Twelve Labours set to Heracles was to clean the Augean stables in a single day. This assignment was intended to be both humiliating and impossible, since the livestock were divinely healthy and therefore produced an enormous quantity of dung. However, Heracles

> succeeded by rerouting the rivers Alpheus and Peneus to wash out the filth. Augeas was irate because he had promised Heracles one tenth of his cattle if the job was finished in one day. He refused to honour the agreement, and Heracles killed him after completing the tasks.

Part Two   Warm-up Questions

1. What do you think of luxury brands? How many luxury brands can you name?

2. Do you want to possess an affordable small stuff of a luxury brand? Why or why not?

3. What do you prefer, shopping online or in a real store? And why?

Section B   Texts Reading

Text A

The Return of Luxury

Top brands are getting back to their core values—and customers. It's about time

http://www.newsweek.com/id/191511
By Nick Foulkes   Mar. 28, 2009

1   It is a pretty depressing business trudging on through this downturn, recession, depression or whatever your euphemism of choice for the financial Götterdämmerung. And in the midst of such overpowering dysphoria luxury might seem to have little point. However, I would argue that these are the times when we most need cheering up with small helpings of the better things that life has to offer.

2   Nevertheless, our relationship with luxury is changing. On the most fundamental level, the very overt way in which we have used our possessions to demonstrate

<u>our status and communicate how we wish to be perceived by others is no longer regarded as acceptable.</u> *The old maxim of nothing succeeding like success needed constant reinforcement through the acquisition of trophies—yachts, jets, art.* The last chairman of Merrill Lynch, John Thain's $1.2 million office refurbishment spree would probably have been regarded as perfectly unremarkable 18 months ago; today it falls somewhere between Imelda Marcos's heroic support of the footwear industry and Nero's musical accompaniment to the flames engulfing Rome.

3 It would appear that an understanding—really, a misunderstanding—developed whereby working long hours and making a great deal of money were equated with virtue. For a while, we all colluded in this status quo, with the world's rich spending their money in a very public way for the entertainment of the rest of us, who looked on as if at some ancient Roman spectacle. The growth of celebrity culture encouraged us to gawp at their excesses and mimic their appearance and habits. We became multilingual experts in brand literacy, and luxury became increasingly regarded as a commodity. For anyone who wanted to get in on it, the grandes maisons de luxe obligingly lowered their entry requirements. If we could not afford the ultraproducts then we were able to start on the nursery slopes. I cannot remember when I first heard the term "entry-level luxury," but I must admit that my heart sank when I did.

4 And I suppose it was this commoditization of luxury that struck me as prima facie, oxymoronic. I am a snob and I like my luxury to be just that: recherché, a little arcane and, quite frankly, not for everyone. Perhaps it is indicative of some psychological frailty in me. However, I understand that this is not good business, and in recent years the luxury sector has boomed in part because of items that were affordable. The brand became an end in itself, assuming a talismanic significance.

5 Take for instance Louis Vuitton. Monsieur Vuitton was a maker of luggage in 19th-century Paris, and it would be interesting to pinpoint exactly when Louis Vuitton's reputation for ingenious, practical and elegant luggage was overtaken by the power of the brand, now associated with a wide range from products, from change purses to high fashion. When a brand breaks out of its comfort zone, it has to work harder to convince the customer that its products beyond its area of expertise have le-

gitimacy. Vuitton is in the enviable position of having started out on this journey of conquest of new spheres of operation many years ago. Nevertheless, its current advertising campaign—featuring a Panama-hatted Sean Connery with a tropical island in the background and the strap line "There are some journeys that turn into legends"—shows how, in difficult times, it is keen to stress its authenticity and return to what in marketing speak is called "core competency."

6   The same is true in a sector that has been very badly affected by the financial downturn: the luxury-car market. Bentley is a marque that I have long respected; I have written two books about its cars and the men and women who drove them. For a while I even wrestled with ownership of one, a fabulous black vintage turbo, before realizing that I was unequal to the financial struggle. Bentley's chairman, Dr. Franz Josef Paefgen, tells me he is dealing with the financial crisis by returning to what the marque is known for. In Bentley's case it means using a unique set of skills to make cars that have a hand-built personality, rather than investing in research to develop new technological gimmickry. Of course Bentley will make use of the latest technical expertise available ... but only insofar as it is consistent with the character of the brand. "We have to deliver what our customers are looking for and not create technologies which are then searching for customers that want them," he says. Increasingly, this is the sort of line that luxury companies need to take if they want to emerge from the current crisis intact. In short, it will be a process of realigning products with the heritage and reputation of the brand—making them special in their own way rather than embarking on programs of brand extension.

7   Until the end of last year, currency was still being given to the idea that there is a stratum of society that is somehow recession-proof. This notion is now discredited, not least because even those who do have it certainly do not want to be caught flaunting it; thoughts of Marie Antoinette and cakes spring to mind. But I have picked up anecdotal evidence that there is activity at the very acme of the luxury pyramid. The other day I was speaking to Jean Claude Biver, the boss of watch brand Hublot, who noted that though it is impossible to escape the effects of the crisis, timepieces costing more than 100,000 Swiss francs are proving less difficult to sell than the more affordable products. I also heard from Neapolitan bespoke tailor Mariano Rubinacci

that some of his wealthiest individual clients have been in touch with him to order new clothes.

8   The truth is that once we have digested the psychological impact of the crisis, and once we have counted the financial cost, we will again be faced with the realities of human nature. It has been true from the time that man first garnished the neck of his cave-mate with a necklace of animal teeth that we have liked, on occasion, to reward ourselves and those we love with items we do not really need. "Why should someone buy another diamond ring for their wife or fiancée?" asks Caroline Scheufele, co-president of the jeweler Chopard, rhetorically. "Of course you have those who were not hurt, and they are in love, and they are going to buy a nice ring for their future wife."

9   A hunger for luxury is a human instinct; it's just that our appetites got out of check. There will be a period of readjustment, an Augean clearing of the branded bric-a-brac that came to clutter our lives and obscure from view the beauty of true luxury. Luxury works a kind of magic on us, but only if we allow it to be special and rare rather than quotidian and readily available. I remember once suggesting to Anne-Marie Colban, proprietress of the legendary Parisian chemisier Charvet, that she should think about appointing a distributor for her eaux de cologne. She looked mildly pained and said something along the lines of "But then it would become too available." She understood that over-familiarity breeds the risk of stripping luxury of its power through banalization.

10 It was Stendhal who said "Beauty is nothing other than the promise of happiness," and the same can be said of luxury. However, I prefer the rather more cynical observation made in a wonderfully wry film called "Nothing but the Best." Made in 1964, it stars Alan Bates as an ambitious young man on the make, who gives voice to one of life's eternal truths: "Face it; it's a filthy stinking world, but there are some smashing things in it." I liked it so much that I had it translated into Latin and made it the motto of a quarterly newspaper I edit called Finch's Quarterly Review. And as the world has turned particularly filthy and stinking, we need those smashing things more than ever.

Text B

Shop After You Drop

Television networks want remote controls to become shopping trolleys

http://www.economist.com/businessfinance/displaystory.cfm?story_id=14587718

From *The Economist* Oct. 8, 2009 / New York

1 Interactive television advertising, which allows viewers to use their remote controls to click on advertisements, has been touted for years. Nearly a decade ago it was predicted that viewers of "Friends", a popular sitcom, would soon be able to purchase a sweater like Jennifer Aniston's with a few taps on their remote control. "It's been the year of interactive television advertising for the last ten or twelve years," says Colin Dixon of Diffusion Group, a digital-media consultancy.

2 So the news that Cablevision, an American cable company, was rolling out interactive advertisements to all its customers on October 6th was greeted with some scepticism. During commercials, an overlay will appear at the bottom of the screen, prompting viewers to press a button to request a free sample or order a coupon or a catalogue. Cablevision hopes to allow customers to buy things with their remote controls early next year.

3 Television advertising could do with a boost. Spending fell by 10% in the first half of the year. The proliferation of digital video recorders (DVRs), now in more

than 30% of households, has caused advertisers to worry that their commercials will be skipped. Some are turning to the internet, which is cheaper and offers concrete measurements like click-through rates—especially important at a time when marketing budgets are tight. With the launch of interactive advertising, "many of the dollars that went to the internet will come back to the TV," says David Kline of Cablevision. Or so the industry hopes.

4   In theory, interactive advertising can engage viewers in a way that 30-second spots do not. Viewers can enter sweepstakes, find nearby shops and play branded games. Unilever recently ran an interactive campaign for its Axe deodorant, which kept viewers engaged for more than three minutes on average.

5   The amount spent on interactive advertising on television is still small. Magna, a unit of Interpublic Group, an advertising conglomerate, reckons it will be worth about $138m this year. That is a far cry from the billions of dollars people once expected it to generate. But DirecTV, Comcast and Time Warner Cable have all invested in it. A new effort led by Canoe Ventures, a coalition of leading cable providers, aims to make interactive advertising available across America later this year. Bright-Line iTV, which designs and sells interactive ads, says interest has surged: it expects its revenues almost to triple this year. BSkyB, Britain's biggest satellite-television service, already plies 9m customers with interactive ads.

6   Yet there are doubts whether people watching television, a "lean back" medium, crave interaction. Click-through rates have been high so far (around 3%—4%, compared with less than 0.3% online), but that may be a result of the novelty. Interactive ads and viewers might not click.

Section C   After Reading

I. *Vocabulary Builder*

1. Read through Text A and B and find the English counterparts of the following Chinese words or phrases.

The following items are for Text A:

1) 显示身份地位
2) 办公室大翻新
3) 音乐伴奏
4) 名人文化
5) 多语言专家
6) 入门级奢侈品
7) 零钱包
8) 高档时装
9) 广告宣传活动
10) 热带岛屿
11) 广告词
12) 用市场营销的行话说
13) 订制裁缝
14) 人类本能
15) 名牌小物

The following items are for Text B:

16) 遥控器
17) 流行情景剧
18) 免费样品
19) 索要优惠券或产品目录
20) 点击率
21) 营销预算紧张
22) 联合利华
23) （身体）除臭剂
24) 广告集团公司

2. Complete the sentences using words given in the box, change forms when necessary.

coalition	crave	collude	currency
intact	obscure	obliging	pinpoint
proliferation	prompt	trudge	wrestle

1) Mother walked the four miles to the nearest store, _____ back home with her bags of groceries.

2) There is plenty of evidence to suggest that many other artists are _____ official approval.

3) This _____ collapsed, however, and a new government was formed in September 1988.

4) Shortening product life cycles and rapid product _____ mean that investment in innovation is critical in global competition.

5) Officials are amazed that the exhibition has _____ so much interest in the public.

6) Recent successes have _____ the fact that the company is still in trouble.

7) The china teacups have to be _____ in their original boxes or they're not worth anything.

8) Legalizing marijuana (大麻) is a concept that has gained _____ in recent years.

9) His jaw was broken while he tried to _____ with a drunken bus driver.

10) The shop assistants were very _____, and brought me at least fifteen pairs of shoes to try on.

11) Several customs officials have been accused of _____ with drug traffickers.

12) Google Earth can help you to _____ the exact location of the hotel in a foreign country.

II. Sentence Translation

1. On the most fundamental level, the very overt way in which we have used our possessions to demonstrate our status and communicate how we wish to be perceived by others is no longer regarded as acceptable. (Para. 2, Text A)

   _____

   _____

2. The old maxim of nothing succeeding like success needed constant reinforcement through the acquisition of trophies—yachts, jets, art. (Para. 2, Text A)

   _____

   _____

3. For a while, we all colluded in this status quo, with the world's rich spending their money in a very public way for the entertainment of the rest of us, who looked on as if at some ancient Roman spectacle. (Para. 3, Text A)

   _____

   _____

4. The brand became an end in itself, assuming a talismanic significance. (Para. 4, Text A)

   _____

5. This notion is now discredited, not least because even those who do have it certainly do not want to be caught flaunting it; thoughts of Marie Antoinette and cakes spring to mind. (Para. 7, Text A)

III. Comprehension of the Texts

Answer the following questions, or choose the best answer.

Questions 1—13 are for Text A:

1. The phrase "financial Götterdämmerung" in Paragraph 1 doesn't mean _____.
   A. downturn   B. recession
   C. depression   D. disaster

2. The subject of the underlined sentence in Paragraph 1 is _____.
   A. midst   B. dysphoria
   C. luxury   D. might

3. The main idea of Paragraph 1 is in the _____.
   A. first sentence   B. second sentence
   C. third sentence   D. nowhere in this paragraph

4. The main verb of the underlined sentence in Paragraph 2 is _____.
   A. have used   B. demonstrate
   C. be perceived   D. is regarded

5. The subject of the italic sentence in Paragraph 2 is _____.
   A. The old maxim   B. success
   C. constant reinforcement D. acquisition of trophies

6. Why are two characters Imelda Marcos and Nero mentioned in Paragraph 2?

7. The topic sentence of Paragraph 2 is "our relationship with luxury is changing". And what's our old and new relationship with luxury respectively?

8. How does luxury become increasingly regarded as a commodity? (Paragraph 3)

9. In Paragraph 5, the author talks about Louis Vuitton's changing brand develop-

ment strategy to adjust to the present recession. What are the old strategy and the new one respectively?

10. What is the new strategy the luxury car brand Bentley takes to adapt to the recession?
11. Does the author agree with the opinion that "there is a class in our society that is somehow recession-proof"? And how does he prove his viewpoint?
12. What is the real subject of the underlined sentence in Paragraph 8?
13. What is the main idea of Paragraph 8?

Questions 14—18 are for Text B:

14. What is the topic of this news article?
15. Which company is going to launch interactive advertisements?
16. Why did the sales of traditional TV advertising decrease from January to June of 2009?
17. Why are the names of many companies mentioned in Paragraph 5?
18. Why do some people hold a negative attitude toward interactive TV advertising?

Unit 15
Gun Control

Section A Before Reading

Part One   Lead-in

The Washington Times is a daily broadsheet newspaper published in Washington, D. C. It was founded in 1982 by Unification Church founder Sun Myung Moon. The political views of *The Washington Times* are often described as conservative. *The Washington Post* reported: "... the *Times* was established by Moon to combat communism and be a conservative alternative to what he perceived as the liberal bias of *The Washington Post.*" However, since January 2008, primarily due to the new editor-in-chief John F. Solomon, who is known for his work as an investigative journalist for the Associated Press and *The Washington Post*, within a month the *Times* changed some of its style guide to conform more to mainstream media usage. The *Times* announced that it would no longer use words like "illegal aliens" and "homosexual," and in most cases opt for "more neutral terminology" like "illegal immigrants" and "gay," respectively. The paper also decided to stop using "Hillary" when referring to Senator Hillary Clinton, and the word "marriage" in the expression "gay marriage" will no longer appear in quotes in the newspaper. These changes in policy drew criticism from some conservatives. Prospect magazine said: "The Republican right may be losing its most devoted media ally."

An editorial, also called a **leading article**, is a piece of writing intended to promote an opinion or perspective. Editorials are featured in many newspapers and magazines, usually written by the senior editorial staff or publisher of the publication. Additionally, most print publications feature an editorial, or letter from the editor, sometimes followed by a Letters to the Editor section. The American Society of Magazine Editors has developed a list of editorial guidelines, to which a majority of American magazine editors commonly adhere.

Part Two Warm-up Questions

1. What's the difference between Chinese and American gun laws?
2. What are the causes of American public gun shooting?
3. Do you agree that Chinese citizens should be granted the right to possess guns? Why or why not?

Section B Texts Reading

Text A

Shootings at Fort Hood

After the Horror at Home

Is there any lesson to be drawn from the shootings at Fort Hood?

http://www.economist.com/world/unitedstates/displayStory.cfm?story_id = 14832025&source = features_box2

From Economist.com Nov.7, 2009 / Texas

1   Fort Hood is one of the largest army bases in America, sprawling over more than 300 square miles (some 780 square kilometres) of nondescript central Texas grassland between Austin and Waco. It is home to more than 50,000 active-duty soldiers, many of whom pass through on their way to Iraq or Afghanistan. One of their errands before deploying is to stop at the Soldier Readiness Processing Centre for last-minute medical and dental checks. It was here, on Thursday November 5, that soldiers preparing for and returning from war encountered a tragedy no one expected.

2 Early in the afternoon a major, Nidal Malik Hasan, who worked as an army psychiatrist, walked into the centre and opened fire with two weapons. He shot dozens of people before Kimberly Munley, a civilian police officer serving on the post, shot him. The bloody rampage lasted for about 10 minutes: 13 people died of their injuries and 28 more were wounded, including Ms Munley. For several hours the based was locked down and plunged into confusion, amid misplaced fears that more than one gunman was at large. Most of the dead were young soldiers. Five had been specially trained to deal with stress among soldiers in combat.

3 It could have been worse. At a press conference the commander of the base, Lieutenant General Bob Cone, praised soldiers who had offered help to the injured and singled out Ms Munley, who had been the only armed person at the scene, for her bravery in stopping the killer. Although the soldiers were unarmed, they had the benefit of their training. One military policeman described arriving on the scene to find Major Hasan unconscious on the floor as unhurt soldiers attempted to help the victims. Many of the doctors and nurses present had earlier been deployed to Iraq or Afghanistan and therefore had experience working in mass casualty mode.

4 After the shootings, details emerged about Major Hasan. His parents were from Palestine, but he was raised in Virginia. He was scheduled to deploy for the first time later this month, to Afghanistan. A cousin told *The New York Times* that he was "mortified" by the idea of going to war and was desperate to avoid it. Religion quickly cast its long shadow over the discussion: another relative said that the gunman had been harassed for being a Muslim, and there were reports that the FBI had been investigating blog posts attributed to "Nidal Hasan" that praised suicide bombers and compared them to war heroes.

5 Elsewhere, Americans were grasping for explanations. The most likely is that the killer was merely a deranged and isolated individual. But right-wing bloggers and

talk-radio hosts have focused on his religion: he had stopped in a convenience store dressed in a traditional white robe and hat on the morning of the attack, and there were reports that he had yelled "Allahu Akbar" before the shootings. Another interpretation suggests that Major Hasan was suffering from the stressful experience of military service during wartime, even if the psychiatrist had not, yet, been deployed into combat.

6 Now questions will be asked afresh about army morale, and about systems for providing support to troubled individuals. Suicide rates among American soldiers are rising, and the Pentagon has promised $50m to a study that is attempting to answer why. At the same time Barack Obama is mulling army operations in Afghanistan. He will soon announce his strategy for the war in that country, responding to a request from his generals for an additional force of perhaps 40,000 soldiers to be deployed. With one war winding down in Iraq and another in Afghanistan bringing gloomier news by the day, the army also must think again how it should cope with some dreadful anxieties among its soldiers at home.

Text B

Editorial: False reports about guns

CBS and MSNBC Peddle Phony Stories about Arms, Race and Violence

http://www.washingtontimes.com/news/2009/aug/31/false-reports-about-guns/? feat = home _ top5_read

From *The Washington Times* Aug. 31, 2009

1 Many media outlets have misfired about guns. Countless newspapers and television networks—from CBS to MSNBC—have misreported that conservative protesters are threatening President Obama with guns at public events. It hasn't happened.

2 In Portsmouth, N.H., a man carrying a gun, William Kostric, joined an Aug. 11 health care protest. This was blocks away and hours before Mr. Obama's town-hall meeting in that city. Mr. Kostric was given permission to be on church property

where the protest occurred and was not at the place the president visited. What most of the coverage left out was that Mr. Kostric didn't carry his gun only for the protest; he legally carries a gun with him all the time for protection.

3   While the media regularly used terms such as "hotheads" to mischaracterize the situation, the coverage ignored that union members who opposed the protest had attacked Mr. Kostric and a friend, kicking, pushing and spitting on them. Despite violence against him by Mr. Obama's supporters, Mr. Kostric did not draw his gun or threaten anyone.

4   On the CBS Evening News, Katie Couric asked, "Are we really still debating health care when a man brings a handgun to a church where the president is speaking?" Deliberately or not, she got the facts wrong. As we know, Mr. Kostric did bring a gun to the church, but the president was not there and never was scheduled to speak there. Mr. Obama spoke at a separate event at a local high school at a different time. Not letting facts get in the way of her hysterical story line, Ms. Couric linked Mr. Kostric's gun to "fear and frankly ignorance drown[ing] out the serious debate that needs to take place about an issue that affects the lives of millions of people."

5   In another case in Arizona, a black man staged an event with a local radio host and carried a semiautomatic rifle a few blocks away from another Obama town-hall meeting. According to the radio station, the staged event was "partially motivated to do so because of the controversy surrounding William Kostric." This occurrence was not an example of an outraged gun-toting Obama protester, but a stunt to garner attention for a shock jock. Of course, this inconvenient truth was ignored by most news outlets.

6   MSNBC misrepresented the facts to try to back up a bogus claim about racism being behind opposition to Mr. Obama's agenda. On Donny Deutsch's Aug. 18 show about the Arizona town-hall meeting, the producers aired a clip of the anonymous black man carrying the so-called assault rifle—but the network edited the tape so the man's race was obscured. Truth be damned, MSNBC anchor Contessa Brewer said, "There are questions whether this has a racial overtone. I mean, here you have a man of color in the presidency and white people showing up with guns strapped to their waists." Another commentator on the same show worried about the "anger a-

bout a black person being president." The supposed result: "You know we see these hate groups rising up."

7   MSNBC's irresponsible behavior is more than just bad journalism; it sows distrust between races. Ernest Hancock, the radio host who staged the event, was hoping to get some free publicity for himself and his show. Whatever one thinks of this PR stunt, it had nothing to do with race. MSNBC misrepresented a black man carrying a gun as a white man to invent a racial dynamic that didn't exist.

8   Media disinformation about guns is a sad sign of the drastic action liberals will take to undermine support for gun rights for law-abiding citizens. It's also an indication of liberals' extreme desperation as Mr. Obama's agenda unravels.

Section C After Reading

I. *Vocabulary Builder*

1. Read through Text A and B and find the English counterparts of the following Chinese words or phrases.

   The following items are for Text A:
   1) 现役军人
   2) 精神病医师
   3) 陷入困惑
   4) 陆军中将
   5) 点名(表扬)
   6) 人体炸弹
   7) 便利店
   8) 士气
   9) 美国国防部

   The following items are for Text B:
   10) 媒体
   11) 市政厅会议
   12) 工会成员
   13) 计划(做某事)
   14) 半自动步枪
   15) 播放一段视频
   16) (电视、电台节目)主持人
   17) 免费宣传
   18) 守法公民

2. Complete the sentences using words given in the box, change forms when necessary.

encounter	indication	misfire	mortified
on the rampage	plunge	single	sow
stunt	undermine		

1) The US was accused of _____ international efforts to combat global warming.

2) The government has _____ strong opposition over its plans to build a new airport.

3) The two parties have shown every _____ of a willingness to compromise.

4) The hunger strike is thought to be just another political _____.

5) After the match, supporters of the losing side went _____ and damaged several parked cars.

6) This would hit struggling homebuyers and businessmen, _____ Britain deeper into recession.

7) His teacher was always _____ him out, calling on him when his hand wasn't even raised.

8) Deaver was _____ by his mistake and immediately admitted that he was wrong.

9) So long as our relationship is defined by our differences, we will empower those who _____ hatred rather than peace, those who promote conflict rather than the cooperation that can help all of our people achieve justice and prosperity. (Obama's Cairo speech)

10) An entire military operation may be adversely affected if a few shells _____ on the battlefield at a critical moment.

II. Sentence Translation

1. For several hours the based was locked down and plunged into confusion, amid misplaced fears that more than one gunman was at large. (Para. 2, Text A)

_____

_____

2. He will soon announce his strategy for the war in that country, responding to a re-

quest from his generals for an additional force of perhaps 40,000 soldiers to be deployed. (Para. 6, Text A)

3. With one war winding down in Iraq and another in Afghanistan bringing gloomier news by the day, the army also must think again how it should cope with some dreadful anxieties among its soldiers at home. (Para. 6, Text A)

4. Not letting facts get in the way of her hysterical story line, Ms. Couric linked Mr. Kostric's gun to "fear and frankly ignorance drown[ing] out the serious debate that needs to take place about an issue that affects the lives of millions of people." (Para. 4, Text B)

5. This occurrence was not an example of an outraged gun-toting Obama protester, but a stunt to garner attention for a shock jock. (Para. 5, Text B)

III. Comprehension of the Texts

Answer the following questions.

Questions 1—4 are for Text A:
1. Where and when did the shooting happen?
2. Who turned out to be the chief trouble-shooter?
3. What advantages do the people at the presence of the crime scene hold?
4. What are three major explanations to Hasan's violent behavior?

Questions 5—8 are for Text B:
5. What has been misreported by CBS and MSNBC?
6. Why does the editor of *The Washington Times* regard the news about Mr. Kostric a misreported one?

7. *The Washington Times* and an Arizona local radio hold different opinions toward the rifle-carrying black man. What are their opinions respectively?

8. What is the purpose for MSNBC to distort the news?

Unit 16
Psychology

Section A Before Reading

Part One   Lead-in

The Virginia Tech massacre was a school shooting that took place on April 16, 2007 on the campus of Virginia Polytechnic Institute and State University (Virginia Tech) in Blacksburg, Virginia, United States. In two separate attacks, approximately two hours apart, the perpetrator, Seung-Hui Cho, a senior English major at Virginia Tech who had previously been diagnosed with a severe anxiety disorder, killed 32 people and wounded many others before committing suicide. The massacre is the deadliest peacetime shooting incident by a single gunman in United States history, on or off a school campus.

The attacks received international media coverage and drew widespread criticism of U. S. laws and culture. It sparked intense debate about gun violence, gun laws, gaps in the U. S. system for treating mental health issues, the perpetrator's state of mind, the responsibility of college administrations, privacy laws, journalism ethics, and other issues. Television news organizations that aired portions of the killer's multimedia manifesto were criticized by victims' families, Virginia law enforcement officials, and the American Psychiatric Association.

An assistant professorship is an entry level position for new PhD graduates. He/she must work hard to produce enough research publications to obtain his/her tenure, like passing a probation. An associate professor has passed his tenure (probation) and is a full time permanent staff, though his position is still junior. A professor is a tenure permanent full time staff and is more senior by promotion.

Part Two Warm-up Questions

1. Have you ever lied in your life? And why do you lie?

2. What do you think of the white lie?

3. Do you often share your sadness and worries with your family or close friends? Does it work? Give at least one example to illustrate your viewpoint.

Section B Texts Reading

Text A

Why We Lie So Much

http://www.time.com/time/health/article/0,8599,1917215,00.html
By Eben Harrell Aug. 19, 2009

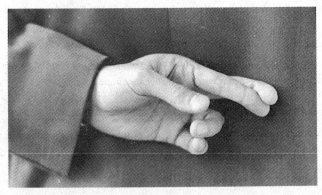

1   A professor of psychology at the University of Massachusetts, Robert Feldman has spent most of his career studying the role deception plays in human relationships. His most recent book, *The Liar in Your Life: How Lies Work and What They Tell Us About Ourselves*, lays out in stark terms just how prevalent lying has become. He talked to *TIME* about why we all need a dose of honesty.

2   **What are the main findings of your research?**

     Not only do we lie frequently, but we lie without even thinking about it. People lie while they are getting acquainted an average of three times in a 10-minute period. Participants in my studies actually are not aware that they are lying that much until they watch videos of their interactions.

3   **One of the reasons people get away with so much lying, your research suggests, is that we are all essentially dupes. Why do we believe so many lies?**

This is what I call the liar's advantage. We are not very good at detecting deception in other people. When we are trying to detect honesty, we look at the wrong kinds of nonverbal behaviors, and we misinterpret them. The problem is that there is no direct correlation between someone's nonverbal behavior and their honesty. "Shiftiness" could also be the result of being nervous, angry, distracted or sad. Even trained interrogators [aren't] able to detect deception at [high] rates. You might as well flip a coin to determine if someone is being honest.

4   What's more, a lot of the time, we don't want to detect lies in other people. We are unwilling to put forward the cognitive effort to suspect the veracity of statements, and we aren't motivated to question people when they tell us things we want to hear. When we ask someone, "How are you doing?" and they say, "Fine," we really don't want to know what their aches and pains are. So we take "Fine" at face value.

5   **Do you feel deception is a particularly relevant topic to our society?**

We are living in a time and culture in which it's easier to lie than it has been in the past. The message that pervades society is that it's O.K. to lie—you can get away with it. One of the things I found in my research is that when you confront people with their lies, they very rarely display remorse. Lying is not seen as being morally reprehensible in any strong way.

6   You can make the assumption that because it often makes social interactions go more smoothly, lying is O.K. But there is a cost to even seemingly benign lies. If people are always telling you that you look terrific and you did a great job on that presentation, there's no way to have an accurate understanding of yourself. Lies put a smudge on an interaction, and if it's easy to lie to people in minor ways, it becomes easier to lie in bigger ways.

7   **You say in the book that recent DNA evidence suggests that 10% of people have fathers other than the men they believe conceived them. So is lying pretty widespread in our intimate lives too?**

Research shows we lie less to people that we are close to. But when we do, they tend to be the bigger types of lies. And the fallout is greater if the deception is discovered.

8   **You show how lying is a social skill. Does that mean it's part of an evolutionary legacy?**

I don't think lying is genetically programmed. We learn to lie. We teach our kids to be effective liars by modeling deceitful behavior.

9   **In your book, you offer a way to cut back on lies. What's the "AHA!" remedy?**

AHA! stands for *active honesty assessment*. We need to be aware of the possibility that people are lying to us, and we need to demand honesty in other people. Otherwise we will get a canned affirmation. At the same time, we have to demand honesty of ourselves. We have to be the kind of people who don't tell white lies. We don't have to be cruel and totally blunt, but we have to convey information honestly. The paradox here is that if you are 100% honest and blunt, you will not be a popular person. Honesty is the best policy. But it's not a perfect policy.

Text B

Let's Not Talk About It

A new study reports that sharing your feelings after a trauma may not always be the best medicine

http://www.newsweek.com/id/139868

By Sarah Kliff   June 3, 2008

1   Like many Americans, Mark Seery watched the Virginia Tech school shooting unfold on the cable news networks in April 2007. It wasn't just the catastrophe that disturbed him—it was how some psychologists were advising the campus community

to respond in the wake of the devastating tragedy. "There's a sense that's very much alive within the professional community that if people don't talk about what they're feeling, and try and suppress it that somehow it will only rebound down the road and make things worse," says Seery, an assistant professor of psychology at the University of Buffalo.

2 That, says Seery, is one of many examples of situations in which the first response to a tragedy's psychological ramifications is to encourage victims and bystanders to talk about their emotions in the wake of the event. Letting it all out, blowing off steam and getting it off your chest are usually thought of as the healthy and appropriate way to deal with difficult and trying moments, like a school shooting, terrorist attack or other collective trauma. And that idea is constantly reinforced by a battery of television therapists who harp on the importance of sharing your feelings. But is that really the best medicine?

3 Seery's new research offers an alternative to that philosophy. His work suggests that those who do not reveal their feelings in the wake of a collective trauma turn out just fine, if not better, than those who do. The study, to be published in the June issue of Consulting and Clinical Psychology, followed more than 2,000 Americans across the nation as they responded to the terror attacks of Sept. 11, 2001, finding that those who didn't share their feelings turned out just fine mentally and physically.

4 "If the assumption about the necessity of expression is correct, then we should expect those who are failing to share would be the ones to express more negative mental and physical health conditions," says Seery, who admits to initially expecting

a different outcome: that the feeling sharers would be healthier in the long term. "I would have thought that the people who did not want to express, that they would have been worse off."

5   Seery used an online survey to query a national sample about their reactions to the 9/11 attacks, beginning on the day itself. (The study was limited by the fact that the results were self-reported and the participants were self-selected.) The respondents were divided into two groups: those who said they were initially unwilling to talk about their feelings, and the rest. They filled out questionnaires about their mental and physical well-being on the day of the attack, two days later, two weeks later, and then every six months for two years.

6   At the end of the two-year survey period, those who decided not to share their feelings reported fewer related mental and physical problems. That effect was even more pronounced among those who lived close to the tragedy.

7   Seery also found an interesting correlation between the level of sharing and well-being. Participants could decide how much they wanted to report about their feelings on the survey. The written responses they gave ranged from sentence fragments like "Feels terrible" to multiple paragraphs. And, says Seery, there was a correlation between those who wrote the lengthier, more in-depth descriptions of their feelings and those who had worse mental and physical statuses.

8   However, one trauma expert cautions against drawing strong conclusions from a national survey in which many of the participants are not necessarily victims of trauma. While September 11 certainly shocked Americans, that doesn't necessarily mean it was "traumatic" for the entirety of the national sample, says Nina K. Thomas, who chairs the postdoctoral specialization in trauma and disaster studies at New York University. "It was a catastrophic event that he's studying, but it's not clear that it had a traumatic impact in the way that many of us would talk about trauma," says Thomas, who explains that the definition of trauma usually includes particular symptoms of distress, like poor quality of sleep.

9   So it's plausible that many of those who chose not to express their feelings did not have a traumatic experience related to the terrorist attacks. And that, Thomas says, makes it a bit unclear how to determine what the research says about those who

are indeed victims of trauma. Thomas does, however, agree with Seery's notion that trauma victims, not friends or psychologists, are the ones who should determine the appropriate way to react. "The immediate victims of whatever trauma are the ones who are the ultimate deciders about how much sharing or talking is right," says Thomas.

10   Does the study turn conventional wisdom completely on its head, suggesting that it's better to stay quiet in the aftermath of a traumatic event? Not quite. Seery explains that the respondents who felt the need to divulge their emotions started off in a worse mental and physical state in the first place, likely a bit more susceptible to the stress of a collective traumatic event. "The people who were talking were probably more distressed by the event," says Seery. "The initial distress motivated them to want to have some place to talk about it ... whereas people who chose not to talk were less likely to say that they were trying cope." The take-home message, then, is that there is no one right way to react to traumatic events; there is a wide range of normal and healthy responses to tragedy.

Section C   After Reading

I. Vocabulary Builder

1. Do NOT consult the dictionary, and guess the meanings of the underlined words from Text A by the help of one or two sentences.

    1) a. Everyone knows that crime is more ***prevalent*** in big cities.

       b. Flu is most ***prevalent*** during the winter months.

    2) a. ***Dupe*** refers to someone who is tricked by someone else especially so that they become involved in the other person's dishonest plans without realizing it.

       b. Their defence was that they were the ***dupes*** in a high powered enterprise and the real criminals were still out there.

    3) a. Someone who is ***shifty*** behaves or looks as if they are doing or planning something dishonest.

b. What are you looking so **shifty** about—is there something you haven't told me?

4) He was filled with **remorse** for having refused to visit his dying father.

5) a. In those days it was seen as highly **reprehensible** for a young unmarried girl to have a baby.

b. The parents of the abused child demanded her teacher's resignation, saying his behaviour had been **reprehensible**.

6) a. The smell of baked apples **pervaded** the house.

b. The power of their positive thinking is infectious and **pervades** our daily working life.

7) a. It's a **paradox** that in such a rich country there can be so much poverty.

b. There's a **paradox** in the fact that although we're living longer than ever before, people are more obsessed with health issues than they ever were.

2. Read through Text B and find the English counterparts of the following Chinese words or phrases.

   1) 在毁灭性的悲惨事件发生后
   2) 助理教授
   3) 集体性创伤
   4) 治疗专家
   5) 提供另一种选择
   6) (情况)恶化
   7) 填写问卷
   8) 句子片段
   9) 建议不要(做某事)
   10) 直接受害人
   11) 关键信息

3. Complete the sentences using words given in the box, change forms when necessary.

alternative	deceitful	detect	fallout
plausible	relevant	suppress	trauma
unfold	veracity		

   1) The system is so sensitive that it can _____ changes in temperature as small as 0.003 degrees.

   2) The first is whether we tend to accept too readily the _____ and accuracy of media reports.

3) I don't think your arguments are _____ to this discussion.
4) The political _____ of the affair cost him his job.
5) Being deliberately _____ about the Government's policies has become something of a habit for the Labour Party.
6) The Fairley family considered that they dealt with their tragedy very well, because both children afterwards showed no signs of _____.
7) As the case against the series killer _____, the District Attorney is expected to continue playing a leading role.
8) She had had to _____ her feelings for George throughout his long marriage to her sister.
9) If payment is not received within five days, legal action will be our only _____.
10) I need to think of a(n) _____ excuse for not going to the meeting.

II. Sentence Translation

1. We are unwilling to put forward the cognitive effort to suspect the veracity of statements, and we aren't motivated to question people when they tell us things we want to hear. (Para. 4, Text A)

_____

_____

2. That, says Seery, is one of many examples of situations in which the first response to a tragedy's psychological ramifications is to encourage victims and bystanders to talk about their emotions in the wake of the event. (Para. 2, Text B)

_____

3. "If the assumption about the necessity of expression is correct, then we should expect those who are failing to share would be the ones to express more negative mental and physical health conditions," says Seery, who admits to initially expecting a different outcome: that the feeling sharers would be healthier in the long term. (Para. 4, Text B)

_____

4. "It was a catastrophic event that he's studying, but it's not clear that it had a traumatic impact in the way that many of us would talk about trauma," says Thomas, who explains that the definition of trauma usually includes particular symptoms of distress, like poor quality of sleep. (Para. 8, Text B)

_____

_____

5. Seery explains that the respondents who felt the need to divulge their emotions started off in a worse mental and physical state in the first place, likely a bit more susceptible to the stress of a collective traumatic event. (Para. 10, Text B)

_____

_____

III. Comprehension of the Texts

Answer the following questions.

Questions 1—6 are for Text A:

1. What is Robert Feldman's field of research?
2. How often do we lie to our acquaintances?
3. Why are we so easily deceived?
4. What is the synonym of "white lie" in Paragraph 6?
5. What are the possible damages caused by white lies?
6. What is Feldman's method to diminish lies?

Questions 7—11 are for Text B:

7. What are the psychologists' suggestion that worries Seery?
8. What are the new findings of Seery's study?
9. What research approach did Sheery take?
10. What are the two aspects from which the trauma expert Thomas argues against Seery's research?
11. What is the significance of Seery's study?